Napoleon Unleashed

Napoleon Unleashed

A History of the Revolutionary, Emperor, and Military Genius who Reshaped Europe and Defined Modern Leadership

Aeon History

uxori liberisque

and

to Hanshi and Shidoshi Keane:
arigato gozaimasu

Contents

Introduction

Men of genius are meteors destined to burn so that earth may be lighted. –Napoleon Bonaparte

The wheel of humankind's history is moved by the supreme forces of the masses, but it was one man's ambition to rule the world that unleashed an age of freedom, progress, and tragedy. Napoleon Bonaparte smashed the known world into pieces and used them to build a brand-new era. He was an eagle flying over the chaos; the beat of his wings fanned the flames of war, sparking revolution and leaving an indelible mark on posterity.

Napoleon supported the French Revolution. He did this by leading the revolutionary army and repelling the European legions that had allied to restore the recently demolished *Ancien Régime*. On the ruins of the French monarchy, this young military leader formed enraged rebels and idealistic citizens into an undefeatable army.

After the first outburst of revolution in 1789, about 6,000 officers (60% of the royal troops) had deserted. Nonetheless, by 1791, 70,000 new men had enlisted. They were simple civilians without military training, but they were led by a cunning and stout-hearted commander who quickly garnered the admiration of his followers. Bonaparte was a commander who could turn them into warriors, equaling the strength of the invaders and defending the republic (Rothenberg, 1989).

The echoes of the revolution reached everywhere while Bonaparte's troops conquered Europe. The colonial bonds that linked the American continent with the Spanish and Portuguese Empires were broken after hundreds of years of dominance. The Napoleonic Wars shook the chessboard of the Old World and created a new balance of power, giving the American states the opportunity to grow into their independence (Arnade et al., 1960). While an empire expanded in Europe, people of a continent beyond the Atlantic Ocean could develop a free society.

French revolutionary ideas spread by Napoleon to the European continent awoke nationalist sentiments in the deeply entrenched empires of the East. Populations oppressed for centuries by the Austro-Hungarian and Ottoman Empires learned new ideas about sovereignty and freedom. These nascent independence movements eventually led to the outbreak of World War I. From there, Napoleon Bonaparte's heritage branched and penetrated the 20th century and reached the present.

The Controversy of Napoleon

Rivers of ink have flown to depict the figure of Napoleon. For some, he was a man of superb genius who dragged his era kicking and screaming into modernity. For others, he was a despot with delusions of grandeur who spared neither effort nor blood to pursue personal glory.

Napoleon is indeed a controversial character who elicits debate between admirers and detractors. The former praise his talents and triumphs. Detractors, however, focus on his flaws and defeats. What is the truth? Who was Napoleon Bonaparte?

He once said history is a collection of lies we all agree on. What lies would Napoleon agree on when speaking about himself? Would he introduce himself as a military genius who brought kings to their knees? Or would he confess to being intoxicated by a lust for power?

Most historians insist on pointing out the actions that shaped the destinies of Europe and the whole world, but what do we know about the deep motivations that moved the man before he became a legend? The aim of this book (in part) is to unravel the mysteries of Napoleon Bonaparte's life, intricately linked with the political agitation of his time and the turbulent process of change. Throughout these pages, we shall uncover the enduring impact of his legacy, and we'll take the good with the bad.

This isn't a simple biography with a chronologically ordered list of significant events. Instead, we want to provide a combination of the personal traits of a man with an excellent military and political career, with a thorough and comprehensive description of the context that framed his life, with due tribute to the context that changed after his actions. It is an unbiased description and analysis of the man and the legend (insofar as is possible), with highs and lows, virtues, and sins. It is the story of a man who synthesized human nature with moments of crowning glory, but also humiliating defeat.

The Intent of This Book

In the following pages, we will depict Napoleon's multi-faceted character: as a military and political strategist, as a son of the Enlightenment, and as a man with human appetites who loved and was loved. He was also feared and hated. He built a new concept of leadership and forged his reputation on numerous battlefields, but his footprint was greater than that. He was also a visionary and a statesman who met success, and then failed. He may have overestimated his own strength.

The main purpose of this biography is to provide an accessible introduction to the great Corsican's life and work. It encompasses a rich, detailed, and impartial understanding of one of the most influential and controversial figures in contemporary history. After reading this book, it will be in the power of the reader to decide how Napoleon Bonaparte should be judged.

Napoleon lived in troubled times when the forces of innovation and change fought against the fading sturdiness of an obsolete system that resisted its decay. In the blur of confusion, only extraordinary minds could anticipate the path to a prosperous future. Bonaparte was one of them. The French Revolution and the chain of events that unfolded are key to understanding his role in history. Through these pages, this complex and prolonged process is condensed to provide a clear explanation without omitting any relevant event, cause, or effect.

Of course, it is difficult to render a full lifetime in a handful of pages. It is impossible to reduce Bonaparte's life to one single book; he lived the lives of a thousand men. Nonetheless, this biography has sought to include the most remarkable moments of his prolific and intense life, from the early years in Corsica until his last moments in Saint Helena, following his steps through the aisles of Notre Dame Cathedral, and at the front of his army on the Russian steppe.

A controversial figure like Napoleon Bonaparte can be analyzed from many concurrent perspectives that are easily overlapped. His life and work can't be separated from the complex environment that shaped his career; and that he, at the same time, contributed to building. While it is impossible to learn the whole history of Napoleon *and* early modern Europe within one single book, there are certain aspects of both realms—the intersection of his personal life with the surrounding social processes—that can't be ignored.

Those aspects have been gathered and are thoroughly explained in the next pages with as much attention as possible. Each chapter is broken down into sub-sections which cover a particular aspect and stage of his life, with the required references to what was happening in the social context. At the end of each chapter, the reader will find a concise summary with key reference points that revisit and refresh the memory of the most relevant moments and point the way to the next chapter.

With these resources and a careful selection of the content, this book is a shortcut to a rich, detailed understanding of one of the most influential military and political leaders of Western history. The facts and processes are a condensed depiction that allows a comprehensive understanding of the highest points of his life as a man and public figure.

Napoleon's Impact

Napoleon Bonaparte can be studied as a man of arms, famous for his strategies in war. He not only led his nation to conquer most parts of Europe, creating one of the most powerful empires in history, but he also deployed unique military strategies that placed him among the great captains of history, perhaps above them. In this biography, we have fairly associated him with the most epic battles, without forgetting the ones where his genius was countered by international alliances, as at Leipzig and Waterloo.

This book will also discuss how his political leadership left an enduring legacy, helping the reader to decode his personal traits and the attributes that made him effective and distinguished him from others. His military campaigns, his meteoric political career, his intervention during the French Revolution, and his ability to build an empire (sometimes by military conquest, but just as often through diplomatic negotiation), have left timeless lessons that deserve to be reviewed.

Even though the most impressive traits of Napoleon are those that made him a great contributor to humankind's history, there is another layer beneath the surface that will also be unraveled: Napoleon, the man. A man who loved and suffered, who was ambitious but also wanted to make his parents proud. He was a man unconditionally admired by his followers and was hated and betrayed by others. Delving into these often less-known aspects of his life, it is possible to achieve a holistic understanding of the person behind the legend.

The name "Napoleon Bonaparte" was a matter of controversy for his contemporaries as much as it is now for anyone interested in him. For some, he should be compared to despotic figures such as Hitler or Stalin, while others revere him as a visionary. Even though it is inevitable to delve into these controversies, the best we can expect is to understand what he did, the possible reasons that led him to make certain decisions, and why he eventually succeeded or failed. Moral judgment is beyond the scope of this volume.

While others might adopt a judgmental position to analyze Napoleon, we aim to present an unbiased perspective. The main objective is to provide a well-rounded view of Napoleon by understanding both sides: his genius, his flaws, and his triumphs and defeats. No matter how many years of research and intense debate we dedicate to Napoleon's legacy, it will never be enough to make a fair trial of the man and the figure. Not even history has been able to judge him; we will not endeavor to do so.

Napoleon was a relevant actor during the revolution that ended the French monarchy. He was also responsible for building a great French empire. Despite his absolute power, he led the reformation of the legal system by creating the Napoleonic Code. While expanding the frontiers of his domains, he spread the ideas of the revolution throughout Europe. This enabled independence movements in distant corners of the European kingdoms.

His reforms irreversibly transformed the feudal structures that persisted on the continent at the beginning of the 19th century. Despite being superstitious, he was an enthusiastic man of science. He promoted a deep reform of the educational system within the empire and was a fierce advocate for public education. He made several significant contributions to science, leading and supporting exploration, archaeological, and discovery expeditions.

His eccentric personality didn't overshadow the brilliance of a statesman. He promoted the modernization of the state and revolutionized the military and financial organization of his country. He hoisted a new global order and a new concept of the balance of power.

Napoleon Bonaparte still captivates people's interest over 200 hundred years after his death. Everything about his life is intriguing, and his legacy remains just as relevant in the present as in the time when he ruled.

Chapter 1: From Corsica to France—The Formative Years

Childhood and Parental Home

How does a boy from Corsica, a mere speck in the Mediterranean, ascend to become the Emperor of France? Perhaps the turbulence of the time when he was born sealed his destiny. The little island was a land of revolutionaries, and Napoleon's early years were a witness to the vicissitudes of politics that significantly influenced his education.

When Napoleon was born, Corsica was a disputed territory. It originally belonged to the Genoese

kingdom but there was a strong independence movement led by Pasquale Paoli. The insurgents sought to
dissolve the bond with the corrupt and archaic Genoese kingdom. Between the 1730s and 1760s, the
island passed through a period of internal crisis, military occupation, and revolutionary war. The
Genoese kingdom was unable to keep the rebellious
islanders under control, and in 1768 the island was
ceded to France for a modest sum.

Napoleon Bonaparte was born on August 15,
1769, in Ajaccio, a small town located on a peninsula
on the west of the island. His original name was Na-
poleone Buonaparte, Italian, since his father Carlo
Buonaparte was descended of Tuscan nobility. His
family had emigrated to Corsica in the 16th century
when it was still an Italian province (Science, Civilization, and Society, n.d.). He was married to Maria-
Letizia Ramolino, a woman of renowned beauty in
the region.

There is extensive controversy among scholars
regarding the time and place of birth of Napoleon. It
is affirmed that Napoleon himself doubted his own
origins. Popular rumors alleged his real father wasn't
actually a Corsican but a Breton (Marlowe, 2020).
Despite the personal interest Bonaparte might have
had to know the truth about his identity, it is fair to
presume it might have had a psychological impact on
him, even as he became a national hero in his future
political and military career.

Despite their noble status, the Buonapartes
weren't a prominent family. Carlo was a lawyer who

just managed to support his family. Nonetheless, he was a man of ambition. Since the times of the revolution, he had been an agitator who joined the forces of Paoli first against the Genoese, and later against the French. Eventually, he set aside his revolutionary impulses to forge a more prominent future for his sons.

In Europe, child mortality in the first years of life was very high. The Buonaparte family had 13 children, though only eight survived. Napoleon was the second of them. His eldest brother, Giuseppe—Joseph, as he was later remembered by history—was close to him. They didn't only share childish adventures in Ajaccio, but later, seized power over a whole continent. When Napoleon became a king, he didn't forget his family; especially his elder brother.

When Napoleon reached power, he appointed his brother Joseph King of Naples between 1806 and 1808. That year, Napoleon employed a diplomatic contrivance to subjugate Western Europe. After removing the monarchs, the emperor named Joseph as the new King of Spain. He remained on the throne between 1808 and 1813. The puppet regency deployed by Bonaparte weakened the Spanish power over its colonies overseas. It was the beginning of the decline of the empire where the sun never set.

Joseph wasn't Napoleon's only brother who would accompany him in his military and political adventures. Their youngest brother, Jérôme, played an important role in Napoleon's strategy to build power in Central Europe. He arranged the marriage of his young brother to Princess Catherine, daughter of the King of Wurttemberg. By then, the territories in the center of the continent weren't under a unified crown. Instead, they were all small principalities.

Employing his siblings was an advantage for Napoleon's pretensions when he didn't find any significant military opposition to his expansion. In such circumstances, he deployed several strategies to gain influence on the different courts. Marriage was a typical political resource to create alliances, and that is what he did with Jérôme. Napoleon created the Kingdom of Westphalia from the northern states of present-day Germany and appointed Jérôme as its king until 1813 (Royal Collection Trust, n.d.).

But during Napoleon's youth, it was a difficult time to raise eight children, so Carlo Buonaparte eased his relationship with the French new authorities. Despite his past as an insurrectionist, he earned the protection of the governor of Corsica who assigned him as a judicial assessor of the town. That enabled him to provide his two eldest sons, Joseph and Napoleon, with a thorough education. The two boys were accepted at the Collège d'Autun, a part of the former University of Paris.

Formative Period at Brienne and Paris

Napoleon was admitted to a military school in Brienne, one of the 12 opened by King Louis XVI for noble boys, because his father presented documents that proved the family's noble origin. However, Napoleon's family didn't belong to a French lineage and his French nationality was questioned. He was often looked down on by his peers and was frequently the butt of jokes, mostly about his lineage or the downfall of his homeland. He was far away from home in a land that didn't welcome him. He became withdrawn and reserved (Chevalier, 2009).

Before reaching the prestigious military school, the two Corsican teenagers had to stay a short while at Autun. They spoke Italian and knew very little French, so they busied themselves learning the language. Shortly after, the two brothers would have to separate. While Joseph remained in Autun, Napoleon continued his way to Brienne.

The military school of Brienne was located in the Champagne region. It was run by the Minimes religious order. Napoleon entered it in 1779 and spent the following five years there. Even though the college was founded to develop military strategy skills, the institution provided a complete educational program that also included a robust course in the sciences.

The curriculum covered exact sciences, language, and history that were especially focused on the art of war. Ironically, Napoleon once called it "the trade of barbarians" (Wheeler, n.d., para. 6). Napoleon was more interested in geography and history. He also proved to be talented in science, arithmetic, and geometry.

With time, he made good use of the knowledge he acquired during those years. He dedicated less time and effort to those subjects he considered useless, such as Latin, as he didn't see any advantage for a soldier to know it. Although he was young, Napoleon quickly learned to discriminate between what was worthy of keeping and what should be dismissed.

Life in a school run by monks wasn't easy for a young boy. Religion played an important role in French society in the late 18th century, and the students were compelled to follow strict monastic isolation. It was particularly tough for a boy who was considered an outsider by the other students and still struggled with the language barrier (Wheeler, n.d.). Furthermore, his life was immersed in the contradictions of being educated by the same nation that had subjugated his own country.

Napoleon never forgot his homeland and its desire for freedom. A nationalist heart beat inside his chest and, on occasion, made him prone to outbursts against the authorities of the school or his classmates. He insulted artwork portraying the French Minister of Foreign Affairs, who had pressured Corsica to surrender to France, and threatened his classmates, saying he would do the French as much harm as he could, probably as a way to defend himself. Once he went so far as to challenge another student to a duel (Wheeler, n.d.).

Despite the adverse circumstances of feeling lonely and excluded, Napoleon developed a temperate character. He spent most of his time in the library. He persisted in his studies and passed his exams successfully. These achievements earned him the chance to continue his studies at a select school in Paris.

He reached the capital of France in October 1784. The *École Militaire* was one of the most prestigious military schools on the continent. A boy with humble origins like Napoleon could only reach there thanks to his own merit. He had earned that place by becoming the 42nd of his class.

During his first year in Paris, Napoleon received news that his father had died of stomach cancer in 1785. Napoleon was only 16 years old, and although he wasn't the oldest son, he assumed the role of being the head of the family. From then on, his efforts weren't only motivated by his personal interest, but were for the sake of his mother and siblings.

Napoleon decided to enter the artillery. He thought it was the best place to develop a career. In addition to his daily military training, he also dedicated himself to studying everything he considered useful on the battlefield: history, philosophy, and geography. During that time, he was in touch with the ideas of Rosseau and Voltaire. The works of these thinkers led him to believe that society needed deep changes, and they played a large part in his later decision to join the French Revolutionaries.

First Military Experience

Despite the bitter first year in Paris, Napoleon once more didn't let circumstances tear him down. He worked hard to accomplish his goals at the school, and within a brief time, he was assigned to his first military post. He proved his skills for leadership on the battlefield and would soon be involved in the events that resulted in the French Revolution of 1789.

Before he had ever moved to Paris, Napoleon had declined the opportunity of becoming a sailor. He had earned the merits to be included in the artillery corps, and that was where he wanted to stay. Within the first year, he was made second lieutenant in the regiment of La Fère, where he continued his training along with other young officers.

Meanwhile, Napoleon didn't withdraw from his intellectual development; he discovered a new facet of his talents. He was sent to a garrison at Valence, and there, he alternated military training with writing. His first notes weren't about military or political issues. Instead, writing was a way to funnel his emotions and frustrations. Although he had finally found a friend in Paris and felt less lonely than in Brienne, Napoleon expressed a thick pessimism in his literary writings.

In his letters, he talked mainly about his longing for his family and his homesickness for Corsica, which he still considered his homeland. One of his first works was entitled *Lettres sur la Corse* (*Letters on Corsica*). He was also concerned about the economic shortage of his family after his father's death and saw in disappointment that his low income as a soldier wasn't enough to support his mother and siblings. In a manuscript dated May 3, 1786, Napoleon ruminated on his own mortality, almost as if he had been planning to take his own life.

His quiet life in Valence was suddenly interrupted by a small rebellion called the "Two-Cent Revolt" that broke out in the city of Lyons in August 1786. Perhaps this call to action took him from the lethargy that brought him dispiriting thoughts. At least there was an occasion to experience the thrill of being on the front lines and find an opportunity to distinguish himself. However, his expectations were quickly stifled.

Napoleon didn't know the background of the events in the rest of the country. All he was told was that Lyon needed the immediate intervention of the royal army. The company Napoleon belonged to left Valence and headed to the site of the upheaval. Regardless of the importance of the event, by the time they got there, the mutiny had been controlled. However, instead of returning to his boring life in Valence, Napoleon was commissioned to Douay, in Flanders.

Unfortunately, from his perspective, his incursion to Flanders likewise didn't garner him any military recognition. On the contrary, he was infected with malaria, which weakened his health for the following years. After a few weeks in Flanders, he returned to Valence, but in August, the Corsican officers were given a free month of leave (Milligan Sloane, n.d.). In September, Napoleon went back home to Corsica.

Upon his return home, Napoleon had to assume his place as the head of his family. His older brother was away, and it was his responsibility to support his mother and ensure the well-being of the younger siblings. During his time at his parent's house, he tried to revitalize the business his father carried out and restore their fragile economic situation. However, his efforts were in vain. He tried with no success to find an occupation in his birth town, and despite his mother's concerns about being alone with the little children, he was soon recalled to his regiment.

In the autumn of 1788, a new tumult arose in the suburbs of Paris. Therefore, many regiments were gathered in readiness for special services, including the garrison of La Fère. Most of the troop was still at Douay by the time Napoleon reached Paris. Therefore, he was appointed to join the royal forces in St. Denis, outside the capital, and later ordered to Auxonne. The social unrest that had caused the disturbance in Lyon had spread, and the king was forced to allow the Estates-General of France to gather for the first time since 1614. It was the sign of an incipient crisis for the monarchy.

Napoleon wasn't concerned about the political frame or the scope of the uprising. By then, his only concern was to make a notable performance that would allow him to be promoted. A military career could take him and his family out of poverty.

Chapter Overview

The first years of Napoleon's life didn't only shape his character but also paved the path for his career, even though he didn't know it at the time. His father's failed ambition to obtain a prosperous life for his sons took the young boy out of his small birth town and gained him a place to cultivate his skills. Entering the army gave him tools to open his way into the rigid French society where social mobility was almost nonexistent.

Furthermore, his time at school broadened his perspective and developed his own motivations for self-improvement. The convoluted environment left in Corsica by its incorporation into the French state engendered a nationalist impulse in the young Napoleon. It would eventually lead him to engage directly in a fight that, at first, wasn't his own.

As Napoleon ventured out of Corsica and delved deep into the heart of France, he soon found himself amidst the whirlwinds of political turmoil. The

French Revolution not only transformed the nation but also heralded the meteoric rise of Napoleon.

Chapter 2: The Spark of Revolution

Impossible is a word to be found only in the dictionary of fools. –Napoleon Bonaparte

The French Revolution

In a nation torn by revolution, a young general's strategic genius would restore order and set the stage for an empire.

The revolutionary process that took place in France didn't start with the fall of the Bastille in 1789, commonly considered the symbol of the beginning of the revolution. Nor did it end with Napoleon Bonaparte's arrival to power in 1799. The causes of the French Revolution need to be traced back in a broader background. Moreover, the revolutionary process demolished a political and social system that had endured for centuries and culminated in a republican regime that executed thousands of citizens. Eventually, it resulted in the first French Empire.

By the end of the 18th century, the *Ancien Régime* that maintained the medieval structure in France was exhausted. King Louis XVI was perhaps the weakest link of absolute monarchy, sufficient to tear the whole system down in continental Europe. The rigid social pyramid that historically divided society didn't correspond with the dynamics of a bourgeoise middle class that developed with the slow but persistent pace of capitalism. The tensions caused by the lopsided distribution of privileges in France could only lead to total destruction.

The Economic Causes of Revolution

The French state was in bankruptcy. Between 1756 and 1763, France was involved in two major armed conflicts: the Seven Years' War, a colonial dispute in North America, as well as the French and Indian War. Both conflicts incurred extraordinary expenses to the crown.

Louis XVI took the throne in 1776. He had to face the consequences of a state with a deep financial imbalance. The situation reached all the social sectors, and social unrest was rising, mainly among the peasants who represented the majority of the population.

Different ministers of finance tried to deploy programs to reduce the state's debt and calm the situation. These programs required new taxes on all the "estates" (socio-economic classes established by the legal order and based on lineage). These were designed to increase the royal income while minimizing expenditures. The goal was to rectify the imbalance in the public budget. Louis XVI refused both measures, and all ministers with similar ideas were dismissed from public office.

Despite the economic problems of the kingdom, the king's wife, Queen Marie Antoinette, continued to lead a lavish life of excess. She was deeply unpopular for her spending on exuberant clothing, sumptuous banquettes, and parties at the palace while the people starved. One might suggest that the queen's standard of living was a compelling reason for the economic distress of the kingdom.

At the very least, it was symbolic, and it was a source of unjustified expenditures in times of scarcity. It was one of the main sources of the monarchy's unpopularity. The ostentatious life of the royal family starkly contrasted with the sacrifices that were demanded of a battered population struggling to survive.

The Social Causes

By the end of the 18th century, French society was divided into three estates. These three estates were based on people's origin rather than their economic condition – they were inherited. This was known as The Estates System, which assigned people different rights and statuses. The estates within this system were the nobility, the clergy, and the Third Estate, which mainly comprised peasants and artisans. The nobility and the clergy were the only two estates with the right of property as a continuation of the feudal conditions of property ownership.

Within the clergy and the nobility, there were significant differences regarding their living conditions. There was an upper and a lower class in each of them. The upper classes had an extravagant way of life, were exempted from paying taxes, and lived on the exploitation of the Third Estate. On the contrary, regardless of the privileges conceded by the Estate System, the low clergy and some impoverished nobles lived in similar conditions to peasants and workers. The Third Estate represented 98% of the total population of France. They also had to pay taxes to sustain the rest of the system (Brooks et al., 2020).

Outside this static social pyramid where nobody could gain or lose privileges, there was a new group that evolved in Europe as trading intensified. It was the bourgeoisie. This was a large group of merchants and bankers who had accumulated wealth but were deprived of the right to become landowners or access political power despite their economic clout.

The Political Causes

The Enlightenment spread ideas questioning the absolute power of the monarchs and advocated for more rights for the common folk. Among the most influential thinkers of the time were Rousseau and Voltaire. They made a great impression on Napoleon during his years as a student.

Rousseau propounded ideas about the social contract that undergirded the states and which made the people the ultimate source of sovereignty. Therefore, according to Rousseau, monarchs exerted power, but it belonged properly to the people, who had a right to claim it back. Voltaire leveled robust criticism against the power and prerogatives of the clergy and advocated for freedom of thought and speech in a regime where expressing against the monarch was considered a crime of sedition (Encyclopaedia Britannica, 2023).

The French Revolution was also influenced by a revolutionary process on the other side of the Atlantic. In 1776, British colonies in North America rebelled against the imperial power of Great Britain. They espoused many of the liberal ideals spread by the Enlightenment.

Within France, the main political catalyst of the revolution was the autocratic power of a king who lacked popular support. He increased the levels of violent repression as the only means to control the crisis in his reign. Meanwhile, there was an increasing request for more civil and political rights led by the bourgeoisie.

Nevertheless, the spark of the revolution wasn't lit by the underprivileged peasants or the rising bourgeoisie, but by the upper classes. In 1787, the new Minister of Finance, de Calonne, levied taxes to be paid by the aristocracy in an attempt to reduce the deficit. The measure awoke immediate reaction from the traditionally privileged sectors and demanded the king to convoke the Estates-General of France.

This was an institution that could only gather if the king requested it. The three estates were represented in the assembly, and each of them held one

vote per deputy, 1200 in total. The result always benefitted the two privileged estates even though the
number of deputies of the Third Estate equaled the
sum of the other two.

When the assembly gathered at the beginning of
1789 to discuss the new taxes, the Third Estate
pressed to impose individual votes. That was the
turning point of the conflict (Brooks et al., 2020).
Since the king refused to accept the measure and instead canceled the Estates-General, the Third Estate
and representatives of the lower classes of the other
estates gathered in Champs de Mars, establishing the
National Assembly. From then on, the conflict esca-
lated, and the revolution unfolded.

The Fall of the Bastille

On July 14, 1789, a mass of peasants—the *sans-
culottes*—and workers from the lower class took their
tools and marched towards the Bastille, a fortress
where political prisoners were incarcerated. Most of
the prisoners had threatened the absolute power of
the king, and for that, the Bastille was a symbol of
despotism. That night, the mob marched, singing the
stanzas of La Marseillaise, and broke down the gates
of the Bastille, marking a flashpoint at the beginning
of the French Revolution. The prison was set on fire
and the political criminals were released.

The event was framed by the *Grande Peur* (Great
Fear). Rumors of an aristocratic conspiracy against
the Third Estate had motivated the peasants to react

against the high class in Paris and the provinces. The gathering of the army around the city alarmed the citizens and fueled the social uprising. The fall of the Bastille is often considered the beginning of the revolution for its symbolic value, and throughout July riots and violence increased (Encyclopaedia Britannica, 2023).

The Constitutional Monarchy and The Terror

The National Assembly continued to meet with the incorporation of members of the other estates. It was declared the National Constituent Assembly and dedicated itself to writing a new constitution for the state. In August 1789, the Assembly declared the abolition of the feudal regime that held the Estates System and diminished the powers of the Catholic church. Later, they also passed the *Declaration of the Rights of Men and the Citizen.*

In 1791, the Assembly attempted to install a parliamentary monarchy where the king shared the legislative and executive powers with a permanent parliament. Louis XVI, advised by his counselors and due to his weak position, accepted. Nonetheless, he and his family were caught trying to escape from France into exile in the Austro-Hungarian Empire where Queen Marie Antoinette came from. The revolutionary forces discovered them and took them prisoner.

By then, the other monarchies in Europe were concerned about the events in France. It was only a matter of time until the revolutionary wave reached them. Austria and Prussia sent military forces to invade France and restore the ancient government.

The foreign attack greatly changed the tenor of the revolution. A new regime was installed to accommodate the changing international political climate. On September 20, 1792, the Assembly was replaced by the National Convention. The new institution declared the abolition of the monarchy and a triumvirate seized power. It was led by the Jacobin leader, Maximilien de Robespierre.

The Jacobins were a political club representing the extreme left wing of the revolution. Their arrival to power brought the installment of the First French Republic. Besides the end of the monarchy, they promoted the universal right to vote (women excluded), the use of the new revolutionary calendar, and the creation of the Committee of Public Safety, an institution that would watch the security of the revolution.

On September 5, 1793, a group of radicals demanded that the National Convention declare "terror is the order of the day" (Encyclopaedia Britannica, 2023, para. 1) Afterward, the government inaugurated a period of extreme political violence that we have come to know as the Reign of Terror. Citizens who were suspected of conspiracy against the revolutionary government, or who belonged to the privileged classes, were imprisoned and later executed.

King Louis XVI, and later his wife, were judged in popular trials and publicly executed by the guillotine. In July 1794, Robespierre was removed from his office and also executed, taking the Terror to an end. By then, about 17,000 people had been killed by the state, and 10,000 died in prison waiting for a trial.

Bonaparte at the Outbreak of the Revolution

Napoleon and his regiment had been transferred to the outsides of Paris in 1788 when the riots began.

However, there was little action where he was, and the troops were taken back to Auxonne. He expected a proper opportunity to prove his courage and skills to fight. However, when that moment arrived, the riot had turned into a mutiny. In July 1789, while in Paris, the revolutionaries tore down the Bastille; outside Paris, the soldiers joined the rebels.

The following months after the outburst of the revolution were filled with chaos and uncertainty. It was difficult to anticipate what course the events would take. However, Napoleon reached two correct conclusions: The Estate System would never be restored, and, without it, all the restraints to ascend in the social scale had been removed. Therefore, the internal crisis of the monarchy opened a new opportunity for the nationalist sentiment of the young Corsican.

With his homeland's independence as the main objective, he joined the Jacobin Club. There, he quickly became one of the most prominent figures. He was the leading voice against the aristocracy and the clergy and all their privileges.

In September 1791, while the country was headed by the constitutional monarchy regime, Napoleon came back to Corsica with the idea of a civil war that would release the island from its conqueror. Even though he attempted to join what was left of the national movement, Corsica didn't have the military power to fight its own revolution. Therefore, Napoleon remained in the French army, which wasn't loyal to the king but to the revolutionary government. The long-awaited opportunity to deploy his military talent was indeed a threat to the French monarchy, but not as Napoleon had imagined. He would fight to defend the revolution from the foreign troops that attempted to restore the monarchy.

The Thermidorian Reaction: Bonaparte's Rising

A year after the beginning of the Terror, the Coup of Thermidor (the 11th month of the revolutionary calendar) overthrew Robespierre from power. It resulted in the arrest and execution of Robespierre and his allies and the end of the Jacobin dominance. Then, a new period of the revolution began: The Thermidorian Reaction.

The new regime installed in July 1794 attempted to moderate the scope of the republican reforms enacted by the Convention and the triumvirate. However, they did this without turning back to the monarchy. The Thermidorian Reaction established The Directory, a collegiate body of five members, and it was a bourgeoisie republic. The most urgent matter at hand was the war against the reactionist European powers that had started in April 1792 and destabilized the revolution.

The Siege of Toulon

Before becoming a national hero for leading the French revolutionary army against the European allies, Napoleon Bonaparte gained fame for the role he played in supporting the revolution inside France's borders. In addition to the menace from abroad, reactionary forces within France tried to give the power back to the Royalists. The rebel group was supplied with arms and resources by Austria and Spain.

The so-called Carmagnoles came from the South, taking cities under control to oppose the revolutionary regime. They had taken the port city of Toulon and prepared to advance on Paris. These Royalists had seized power in the city but they wouldn't resist long alone, so they sought British assistance. For the Republic, recovering the city was vital as it was a key port on the Mediterranean Sea.

By that time, Napoleon was a 24-year-old captain who had been introduced to the army by his Jacobin friends Saliceti and Augustin Robespierre (Mark, 2022). In September 1793, Bonaparte was on his way with a convoy from Marseille to Nice. He decided to stop at the garrison of Carteaux. There, he was appointed commander of the Republican artillery. His mission was to besiege the city of Toulon and force the Royalists to surrender. Napoleon had no experience in battle, but with the confidence of youth, he accepted the mission and approached it as an opportunity to make a name for himself.

His artillery was precarious and many of his soldiers were volunteers to the revolutionary cause. However, Napoleon deployed innovative strategies to fight. He organized his troops into two corps and gave them nationalist names to inspire them: La Montagne and Des Sans-Culottes, making reference to the revolutionary political wing of The Assembly and the protagonists of the Bastille's fall. Then, he formed two batteries on two hilltop forts and bombarded the Allied ships. However, Napoleon's first part of the plan resulted in a terrible massacre of his Republican artillery.

Nevertheless, Napoleon was undeterred, and this time he reinforced his batteries. He displayed strategies never used until then. He sent letters to the neighboring cities calling people to join the revolution and fight against their common enemies. He also sent a message to those who wouldn't support them. He threatened them and forced them to send arms, powder, and horses.

He and his men worked hard for weeks to be ready for the final advance on Toulon. He still needed volunteers, so he used again his innovative strategy to inspire followers. He named the battery *Le Batterie des Hommes Sans Peur* (The Battery of Men Without Fear). Plenty of men joined the artillery.

The maneuver to take Toulon was risky. Part of the Republican artillery was used as bait while the rest crossed enemy lines via a hidden trench. Once inside the Allied battery, they started shooting, causing great confusion among the Royalists. Eventually,

Napoleon gave the order for the last attack and personally led his troops. In the middle of the assault, his horse was killed and he received a bayonet wound in one of his legs. Toulon finally fell in December 1794.

After the capitulation of the Royalists, Napoleon Bonaparte was promoted to brigadier general in recognition of his achievement in Toulon. Back in Paris, he played a key role in saving The Directory. The levels of violence hadn't decreased after the replacement of the Jacobins in power, and the fall of Toulon didn't mean the end of the reactionary attacks.

In 1795, Napoleon was in Paris, and a Royalist mob attacked and killed the guards protecting the Tuileries Palace. On this occasion, Bonaparte didn't hesitate to open fire to disperse the mob (*Bonaparte Saves the Day*, n.d.). It is said he used "a whiff of grapeshot" to control this uprising against The Directory and establish order in the streets. In this way, Brigadier General Bonaparte saved The Directory and earned the government's trust.

Chapter Overview

The French Revolution was the end of the *Ancien Régime*; it was the moment for the bourgeoisie to seize power. However, once the process unfolded, it was difficult to stop. The revolutionaries drove the French to a liberal extreme, while the rest of Europe attempted to restore the absolute monarchy. In the middle of these events, Napoleon found his own path to power.

From the rubble of a revolution, a young general began his ascent, rapidly climbing the ladder of power and influence. But how did Napoleon transition from a successful general to a political leader?

Chapter 3: Rise to Prominence

Napoleon once wrote: "The strong man is the one who is able to intercept at will the communication between the senses and the mind" (*Napoleon Bonaparte Quotes*, n.d.). The chaos unleashed by the revolution required a cold mind and a strong character. Bonaparte proved to have both and to be able to use the obstacles set by the circumstances to his benefit.

In times of such uncertainty and increasing violence, it is difficult to measure the impact of actions. It was a challenge to make hard decisions and stand to face the consequences. After saving the revolution at the siege of Toulon and The Directory in October 1795, Napoleon's influence in the army and government rapidly increased, along with his political career.

By 1796, the internal crisis had been stabilized. A bourgeoisie republic was ensured. All the forces were then concentrated on repelling the attacks from the reactionary European monarchies.

Italian Campaign: Tactics and Leadership

The French revolutionary army had successfully repelled the invasions from the North and the East. The War of the First Coalition began in 1792. After defeating the Netherlands, Prussia, and Spain, the reactionary monarchies were ready to negotiate under the terms of the new French government. However, it still had to pacify Italy. Napoleon was appointed to lead the campaign.

The French revolutionary army led by Napoleon invaded Savoy in 1796 and forced the Austrians to retreat. Then, he advanced to Venice and the Cisalpine Republic. In every principality he reached, he compelled the Austrians to recognize the local authorities and persuaded them to sign a treaty with France.

Thus far, the Italian cities he passed through believed it served their nationalist objectives. They saw Napoleon as a savior from Austrian oppression (Lumen Learning, n.d.). Within a few weeks, Napoleon had conquered most of the Italian principalities with minimal effort, mainly using his diplomatic skills.

When the Italian campaign started, Napoleon was only 26 years old. He reached Nice, his staging point, in March 1796 and found a demoralized and weakened troop close to the point of mutiny: "The men were starving and malnourished, given only meager rations provided by corrupt contractors who charged extortionate prices. They lacked the most basic supplies; muskets, bayonets, and uniforms were all rare commodities and entire battalions went without shoes" (Mark, 2023, para. 4).

He had to struggle with the lack of resources, but especially with the distrust of the men abandoned by the state. The soldiers had to wait for months for their salaries, and (when they arrived) they were bank-notes instead of money. Yet, he managed to rebuild trust and discipline and won the respect of his subor-dinates.

A key element of Napoleon's plan in the 1796 campaign was to divide the opposing Austro-Sardin-ian army. A rousing French cavalry charge at Dego, which scattered an enemy relief column, ensured this result (Lombardy, 2013). On April 2, 1796, Napoleon entered Italy with a 38,000-soldier army. He had to confront the allied forces of Italy and Austrians who numbered over 60,000 men.

Despite the disadvantage of being outnumbered, Bonaparte contrived a strategy to isolate the Austri-ans from the Piedmontese Italians. Once separated, he would attack them in turn. Napoleon defeated the Italians, who then sued for peace. He had conquered Piedmont.

After losing Sardinia and Piedmont, the Austri-ans withdrew. Nonetheless, Bonaparte was determined to push them away from the Italian pen-insula. Therefore, as the Austrian army raced to Milan, he pursued and intercepted them at the town of Lodi.

Lodi was a small Lombard city where the French and the Austrian armies prepared to fight a violent battle. Napoleon crossed the Po River, near Piacenza, to enclose the Austrians in their retreat. On May 10, 1796, the troops met at the bridge where the bitterest part of the combat took place. The French blocked the Austrians' path to Milan and impeded their retreat to Mantua. It ended up in a French victory "Which gave Bonaparte his nickname the 'Little Corporal,' opened the route to Milan, and assured him his conquest of Lombardy. On May 11, 1796, he wrote to Carnot, 'La bataille de Lodi donne à la République toute l'Italie'" (*The battle of Lodi has given the Republic all of Italy*, n.d., para. 1).

Lodi didn't command great strategic significance, but it proved the courage of the French soldiers and earned their leader his people's love and respect. Moreover, it proved Napoleon's determination to himself and his rivals. He later wrote: "I no longer regarded myself as a simple general, but as a man called upon to decide the fate of peoples. It came to me then that I really could become a decisive actor on the national stage" (Mark, 2023, para. 13). It was a turning point in his own perception of himself and kindled his ambition yet further. Afterward, Napoleon and the French army headed to Mantua.

The *Armée d'Italie* under Napoleon's command besieged Mantua, the city where the center of Austrian power in Italy lay. The strategy was to cut the Austrian supply lines. The key was to take Arcole, a small town. If they succeeded, the French could control the road used by their enemy, but failure would mean the end of Napoleon's adventure (NGV, n.d.). However, the Austrians hadn't given up their designs in Italy and sent a large army to break the siege.

The town of Arcole was surrounded by marsh-land. The Alpone River was restrained by dikes 10 meters high placed to halt invaders, but that served Napoleon in his strategy. He ordered his men to scale the dikes with regimental colors. It caused confusion among the enemies and eased the French advance. After three days of intense fighting, the town fell to French hands. The Austrians permanently left Mantua and Italy.

The siege of Mantua and the fight at Arcole were the highest points of Napoleon's campaign to Italy. The city had great strategic importance for the European Allies, particularly Austria, which sought to retain its possessions in Savoy and Sardinia. On the other hand, it symbolized Napoleon's determination to conquer and prevail (Cuccia, n.d.).

Egyptian Expedition: Ambition and Miscalculation

At the late stage of the revolution, France was still struggling with Great Britain. The Directory appointed the young General Napoleon Bonaparte as the commander of the *Armée d'Angleterre*, in preparation of an invasion of England. However, Napoleon had his own plan to decimate the British power.

The key was to reduce their influence on the seas and their colonial possessions in Asia. Therefore, he planned to increase the French presence in the Med-iterranean Sea by taking positions in Northern Africa. In 1798, he commanded the *Armée d'Orient* in an invasion of Egypt, which was under the Otto-man Empire's power (Mark, 2023).

Egypt was a strategic point in international trad-ing routes as it connected the Mediterranean Sea to the British colonies in India. The Nile River was a wa-ter route that linked the Red Sea with the Mediterranean and, through it, with the Atlantic Ocean. On the other hand, the decline of the Ottoman Empire could open a space of expansion for the Brit-ish and the Russians, two major enemies of France. Meanwhile, the local powers in North Africa were a problem for the Ottomans and for the European pow-ers, and Egypt itself had rebelled against Istanbul.

The Battle of the Pyramids

By 1798, Egypt was ruled by the Muslim slave de-scendants of Mamlūks, an oppressive power resisted by the citizens. Alexandria had been abandoned, and the population had to defend itself. In July, Napo-leon's army found no resistance and quickly seized Alexandria. There, the general established a garrison and started a propaganda campaign against the local government. Similarly to what he did in Italy, he wanted to boost his support among the local popu-lace.

Afterward, his army marched toward Cairo. The path between Alexandria and Cairo was extremely challenging and almost caused the failure of the mission. Napoleon organized the expedition in separate columns. The one he led was harassed by Bedouins. The French soldiers were close to starvation. Many of them committed suicide, and many others died of dehydration (Encyclopaedia Britannica, 2023).

Eventually, those who survived approached the west bank of the Nile and fought against the unaware forces of Mamlūks at Shubrā Khīt. There, he obtained a quick victory. On July 21, Napoleon confronted the Mamlūks in the so-called Battle of the Pyramids, also called the Battle of Embabeh. The battle lasted no more than an hour, and three days later, Napoleon entered Cairo, victorious: "His victory was attributed to the implementation of his one significant tactical innovation, the massive divisional square" (Encyclopaedia Britannica, 2023, para. 1).

When General Bonaparte defeated the Mamelukes at the Battle of the Pyramids, he carried out only the first move in a complicated game. The occupation of Cairo was not the main object of this expedition. The central goal was to interfere in Britain's communications with the East, destroy trade, and loosen its grip on India. If it worked well, even a French occupation of part of Australia would be possible.

To the young Corsican-born general, just coming into his stride in the wake of his brilliant campaign in northern Italy, the possibilities seemed to be infinite.

"This little Europe is too small a field," Napoleon sup-posedly said before setting out for Alexandria. "Great celebrity can be won only in the East" (*Battle of Aboukir Bay*, n.d.).

Despite his victory, Napoleon Bonaparte's cam-paign in Egypt didn't end as he expected. He didn't have enough men to occupy all the territory and struggled with local revolts. Meanwhile, he continued to lose men to illness. In 1799, he decided to go back to Paris.

The Scientific Discoveries

Regardless of its limited military success, the campaign to Egypt had other significant outcomes. The main purpose of the mission was martial, but Na-poleon, who had always been keen on history and science, also had a scholarly aim. He wanted to collect information from ancient Egypt, which he considered as important as classical Greece and Rome. There-fore, along with his troops, he took more than 160 scholars and artists. The Commission of the Sciences and Arts of Egypt made a great contribution to his-tory: "Their careful work, carried out over many years, would give birth to the field of Egyptology in Europe and reveal to the world the history of the grand civilization that had ruled along the Nile for millennia" (Molinero, 2021, para. 2).

The French scholars spent three years of the French occupation of Egypt collecting and docu-menting discoveries about the ancient civilization. It was the first large-scale systematic study of ancient Egypt. The French scientific team made a meticulous topographical investigation and provided detailed maps. Among the most important discoveries were the temples and tombs in the Valley of the Kings. Similar structures at Luxor, Philae, and Dendera were measured, drawn, and mapped to depict a pharaonic Egypt hitherto unknown to the European world.

Another outstanding discovery was the Rosetta Stone, written in three different languages, including hieroglyphics. Although there is some debate about the exact date, in 1799, "during Napoleon Bonaparte's Egyptian campaign, a French soldier discover[ed] a black basalt slab inscribed with ancient writing near the town of Rosetta, about 35 miles east of Alexandria" (*Rosetta Stone found | July 19, 1799*, 2009).

Besides historical finds, the French scholars made many other important discoveries in other fields. They had been ordered to collect as much information as possible. Gaspard Monge unraveled the mirage phenomenon, and the naturalist Etienne Geoffroy Saint Hilaire discovered many new types of fish. The artist Henri-Joseph Redouté drew species of flowers and plants that were unknown in Europe. The engineers Jean-Baptiste Prosper Jollois and Édouard de Villiers du Terrage produced many technical drawings of the monuments in Thebes, Karnak, Abydos, and Antaeopolis (present-day Tjebu).

The French also learned about Egyptian practices and machines that were taken by the expeditionary force back to France. One of the most innovative was a type of jar used to keep drinks cold for many days:

> plaster was made up in a mill – making life much easier for craftsmen – whilst France still continued to make it up by hand. Egypt had also developed machines known as "chicken ovens", which served as artificial incubators for chicks and other baby birds (Lefevre & Papot, n.d., para.7).

The discoveries made by the French during Napoleon's campaign provided the Louvre with one of the most important collections of Egyptian objects. All the scientific discoveries, including the Rosetta Stone, made invaluable contributions to the development of science and research with a legacy that endures in the present.

Political Maneuvering and the Path to Power

Napoleon went back to Paris as a victorious general. Despite the military pitfall in Egypt due to a miscalculation of the obstacles that could arise, he had won his battles and the French occupation continued for three years. In France, he was welcomed as a hero.

Meanwhile, political unrest was still heated in the country. Napoleon had the ability to capitalize on his military achievements abroad to overcome internal conflicts. In 1799, Napoleon and his allies overthrew the French Directory government after the Coup of 18–19 Brumaire and established the French Consulate (Clendenin, 2022).

The Second Coalition War between France and the European powers began in 1798. That led The Directory to take unpopular measures like massive conscription of unmarried men to join the army. After the euphoria of the early stage of the revolution decreased, people sought peace. In addition, the levels of corruption in The Directory diminished people's trust in the government.

The turning point of the crisis was when the Royalists won a majority in the Assembly and enacted reactionary reforms. Some of the most vindictive members of the new majority organized a conspiracy to overthrow the unstable and corrupt Directory. They searched for the support of a legitimate figure, and Napoleon stepped forward.

The conspirators, counting on the support of the army lining up behind Bonaparte, obtained the resignation of the members of The Directory and formed a provisional government. The new government passed a constitutional reform to create The Consulate and provide a legal framework for institutional change. Even though the executive power relied upon three consuls, Napoleon was the only one who functioned effectively. It was a bloodless *coup d'etat*.

After the Coup of 18 Brumaire (November 9–10, 1799), Napoleon won a rigged election to the First Consulate, making way for despotism: "Napoleon became 'first consul' for ten years, and appointed two consuls who had consultative voices only. His power was confirmed by the new Constitution of 1799, which preserved the appearance of a republic but in reality, established a dictatorship" (*Napoleon's Rise to Power*, n.d., para. 13). This event is considered the effective end of the French Revolution. For the French, that meant a period of major stability began (Mark, 2023).

Chapter Overview

Napoleon's military career was boosted by his successful campaign in Italy and Egypt during the First Coalition War. There, he didn't just prove his skills as a military strategist, but also his leadership skills. He became a symbol for the French citizenry who saw a hero capable of saving the revolution from the reactionary powers of Europe. And he inspired his soldiers. Napoleon's greatest accomplishment wasn't to defeat the Allied powers but to reorganize the troops that were disorganized and demoralized in Italy, showing he could restore order and discipline. Moreover, these triumphs gave him a new perspective of what he could aim for.

Back in Paris, the need for peace after political instability and 10 years of revolutionary effervescence placed him in the role of the leader France needed to build a new era. His name and reputation as a successful military leader, combined with his innate talent to turn adverse conditions to his own benefit, made him the man chosen on the 18 Brumaire *coup d'etat* to seize power. Then, he started his own revolution.

With the political landscape of France under his control, Napoleon was positioned for even greater feats. But with increased power came greater challenges. In the next chapter, we examine Napoleon at the pinnacle of his power as he assumes the title of Emperor. It's the height of his ambition and influence, and the reforms that would reshape Europe.

Chapter 4: The Pinnacle of Power—Becoming Emperor

I love power. But it is as an artist that I love it. I love it as a musician loves his violin, to draw out its sounds and chords and harmonies. –Napoleon Bonaparte

During the first years of his mandate, Napoleon implemented a series of measures to centralize power. In 1799 he established The Consulate. In 1802, he declared the first Consulate for Life. However, his reformations weren't limited to the increase of his personal power. Instead, he led a profound transformation of the country by setting the basis of a modern state with long-lasting reforms.

He centralized the administration, promoted public education, and created a higher education system. He made great investments in infrastructure to provide the country with roads and a sewer system. In order to fund the state, he created a more efficient tax collection system.

Napoleon also made one of the most important contributions to the evolution of legal systems. He created the Napoleonic Code or French Civil Code. This work produced an analysis and commentary on the existing laws, compiled and organized into a single code.

Before the Napoleonic Code, France didn't have a unified body of laws. Instead, "Law consisted mainly of local customs, which had sometimes been officially compiled into *coutumes,* or customs. There were also exemptions, privileges, and special charters granted by the kings or other feudal lords" (*The Napoleonic Code: Legal System in France before the Code,* n.d., para. 1).

The Napoleonic Code formalized many achievements of the bourgeoisie during the revolution such as equality under the law, property rights, and the abolition of the feudal estate system. Later, Napoleon would take his revolutionary code to the rest of Europe, ensuring the reach of liberal ideas across the whole continent. Even though it wasn't the first legal code to be implemented in Europe, it can be credited as the first modern code with a pan-European scope. Countries like Germany, Italy, and Switzerland (among others) adopted the code, and it had a deep impact on many contemporary legal systems.

Furthermore, it was especially influential in Eastern Europe. This was the last region of the continent to overcome the feudalist structures that left them far behind the political and social progress of the West. The application of the code accelerated the processes of modernization in these nations (*The Napoleonic Code,* n.d.).

Besides the ideological background of the laws, the implementation of the Napoleonic Code was a significant change in the nature of civil law systems. A systematized body of laws made it clearer and more accessible for everybody. Before the reform, there wasn't any legal instrument that compelled the government to publish laws. As a consequence, the government wielded great power over the citizens with the ability to enact laws without communicating them. From the moment the Napoleonic Code was enacted, secret laws were no longer allowed.

The Code also added more transparency to the administration of justice, fundamental for building a new, stable state. It ensured the right to a fair trial and established the mechanisms for more effective functioning of the judicial system for the benefit of the citizens, since:

> It prohibited *ex post facto* laws (i.e. laws that apply to events that occurred before their introduction). The code also prohibited judges from refusing justice on grounds of insufficiency of the law, thereby encouraging them to interpret the law. On the other hand, it prohibited judges from passing general judgments of a legislative value (The Napoleonic Code, n.d., para. 5).

Despite Bonaparte's version of the republic having a strong tendency to centralize power in his hands, rather than observing a separation of powers, the Napoleonic Code was perhaps the first effective reformation to eliminate the reminiscence of absolute monarchic powers.

Centralization of Power, Diplomatic Endeavors, and Modern Politics

The matter of the centralization of power is controversial. On one hand, it seems like the revolution made French society turn its history in a circle, leaving it almost in the same place it was before the Revolution. The new regime was legitimized through a new constitution to preserve the *appearance* of a republic. The Constitution of the Year III (according to the new calendar imposed by The Directory) created a new executive power of three members, but Napoleon Bonaparte became the only one to wield power; the other two were just figureheads. It was a functional monarchy.

The principles of representation and the supremacy of the legislative body, the groundings of any republican system, were discarded. The separation of powers was eliminated. Instead, the power to pass laws was ceded to the executive: Napoleon. The legislative branch was maintained only to preserve the formality of acquiring the signature of the executive, but it lacked any real power of voice or vote. The elections were also maintained, but it was nothing more than elaborate political theater where the voters had no real power of decision (Encyclopaedia Britannica, 2011).

Despite this turn back to a regime very much like the absolute monarchy that the revolution attempted to leave behind, there were several liberal reforms that represented a move forward in the global political system. The Napoleonic Code was a way to formally institutionalize the changes introduced by the revolution to abolish the medieval structures that persisted. The expansion of Napoleon's power over Europe enabled the spread and entrenching of liberal ideals and halted the reactionary counteroffensive of the monarchies that were hampered by those ideals.

On the other hand, the years that followed the revolution had high levels of violence and instability, typical of a process of abrupt and profound destabilization of traditional structures: political, economic, and social. French society was torn down and, at the same time, faced the threat of an external invasion for more than 10 years. In the middle of this chaos, there was a possibility of turning back to an extreme government like the Jacobins' erratic Republic and Robespierre's Reign of Terror. In this context, a strong centralized power could stabilize society, defend the nation's borders, and avoid repeating the terrible experiences France had already been through.

Unlike traditional autocratic powers, Napoleon didn't resort to coercion to control the population. Instead, he used diplomatic methods, as he had deployed to obtain the non-violent surrender of some of the Italian principalities. He also used other means of persuasion to influence public opinion closer to what is called propaganda today.

Napoleon cared to court people's opinions enough to employ efforts to gain their sympathy and support:

> As a shrewd strategist and politician – a master
> of managing appearances to manipulate opin-
> ion – Napoleon realized the potential of great
> works of art to instill in hearts and minds the
> validity and might of the Empire and his au-
> thority to lead (NGV, n.d., para. 8).

During the revolution's early years, French citizens were constantly and systematically bombarded
by the press to manipulate their opinions. The aim
was to consolidate a new sense of loyalty and national
identity linked to liberal ideas. The media consisted
of pamphlets, newspapers, and caricatures published
and massively distributed, but the revolutionary governments also resorted to public monuments and
performances of plays and music.

Napoleon built his career in the heat of this revolutionary process, and he didn't hesitate to deploy the
methods that had been proven efficient. Then, he
"took the Classical revival of the 1790s, originally
used to promote the Republican values of austerity,
citizenship, self-sacrifice, and duty, and used it to
promote his own achievements as Emperor" (NGV,
n.d., para. 8).

Napoleon manipulated all communication media
available at his time to spread his political ideas.
Those media were newspapers, journals, and pamphlets, and also public gatherings, arts, and even
religious services. He used propaganda to increase
the tension or to ease the mood of the multitudes, for
his personal purposes.

For instance, propaganda played a key role in disseminating his triumphs on the battlefield. He expressed confidence and enthusiasm among the French citizens and, later, the nation's allies. The news about his success stood in stark contrast to the negative coverage directed toward his enemies.

Napoleon used the media to consolidate his power and strengthen a new French identity. He effectively motivated citizens to join the French army, and his arrival to power through a *coup d'etat* didn't lack popular support. He discouraged the enemy and swelled nationalist feelings: "He used fear to impose peace, concluded treaties with countries who had seen his power, used the media to spread his message, and worked to prevent or split coalitions" (The Raab Collection, 2019, para. 1).

In the long term, Napoleon developed a system of control over the press. If it had the power to manipulate public opinion, it had to be centralized. It was one of the highest prices paid for order and stability.

The French who supported Napoleon Bonaparte's rise to power had no means to anticipate the consequences of his ambition: the time and lives spent to expand and ensure his kingdom. Despite his irrepressible thirst for power and his aspirations for glory, his arrival and building of power during the time of the Consulate were aligned with the national interest of citizens and embodied the needs of the nation.

Becoming an Emperor

On March 27, 1802, the countries at war with France signed the peace at Amiens. Even Great Britain established peace in Europe. However, they had a common concern. Should Napoleon Bonaparte be a Consul for Life?

In 1802, elections gave Bonaparte the legitimacy he needed. However, it fueled international conflict. The state of war until 1799 took Napoleon to power, and his ability to build peace through diplomatic relationships ensured his role in the Consulate. The new tensions boosted the rise of the empire.

The Treaty of Amiens motivated Napoleon to expand his borders overseas in America, India, and Northern Africa. In continental Europe, France incorporated Piedmont, established a more centralized organization on the Swiss Confederation, and compensated the German princes with lands in the region of the Rhine River. The expansion had begun, and Europe was alarmed again.

Within the country, Napoleon had detractors, many of whom planned to eliminate him by assassination. In 1804, Napoleon discovered a conspiracy financed by the British (Godechot, 2023). Then, the chief of police advised him to turn the Consulate into a hereditary empire. This would discourage conspiracies to kill him since it wouldn't mean the end of the regime. Bonaparte proclaimed the Empire in May 1804.

In most aspects, the empire maintained most of the institutions established by the consulate. However, some employed during the *Ancien Régime* were revitalized. Moreover, Napoleon thought about increasing his legitimacy as a ruler by obtaining the blessing and symbolic support of the papacy.

God and, by extension, the Catholic Church as the divine source of the absolute monarch's power were the foundation of political power during the Middle Ages, and the consolidation of the monarchies from the 15th century on. Predictably, the power of the church was one of the main targets of the French Revolution in 1789. The first revolutionary reforms targeted the Catholic Church's properties and its privileges within the state. By requesting the Pope's blessing, Bonaparte retraced his own steps. However, being consecrated by the pope had a different symbolic meaning for Bonaparte; he wanted to have a more spectacular crowning than the other kings of Europe.

Pope Pius VII agreed to come to Paris to officiate the ceremony. The event was equally rejected by Royalists and Revolutionaries. By that time, their opinion mattered very little. On the other hand, the Pope pursued his own political interests. He agreed to attend the ceremony to gain Napoleon's goodwill and discourage him from attacking Rome and the Papal States (Sparknotes, n.d.).

The crowning ceremony was arranged to be at Notre Dame Cathedral on December 2, 1804. When the moment of putting the crown on the emperor's head came, Napoleon took the crown from the Pope's hands and did it himself. He did so to heighten the importance of his action. By putting the imperial crown on his own head while the Pope stood by, Napoleon made a symbolic gesture stating that he would be subservient to no one on Earth, and that Rome would never command him.

Shortly after, Napoleon Bonaparte crowned himself again as King of Italy in March 1805. In 1802, he had already named himself President of the Cisalpine Republic when France annexed the region through a diplomatic maneuver. From then on, an autocratic regime was fully established. Napoleon created a new imperial nobility and distributed princely titles. He intensified the control of the press and the use of propaganda to exert complete control of public opinion (Godechot, 2023). The regime had mutated into a dictatorship and the appearance of the republican forms wasn't among the emperor's priorities.

Chapter Overview

When Napoleon came back to Paris and established the Consulate in 1799, his name was a synonym for order and peace. Once in power, he unleashed his ambitions and sped up his race for absolute power. He ensured internal unity and negotiated peace with most of his enemies in Europe. He had popular support and was astute enough to use all the resources of coercion and politics to accommodate circumstances to his own desires.

As Napoleon sat atop his self-made throne, Europe watched closely. His ambitions didn't stop at France. They extended far and wide, seeking to reshape the very essence of the continent. But as he ventured outwards, the stakes got higher.

Chapter 5: The Grand Empire and Continental Europe

In war, the moral is to the physical as three is to one. –Napoleon Bonaparte

France's expansion commenced during the Consulate period through diplomatic efforts, such as the annexation of Piedmont. Simultaneously, the groundwork for future actions, like those involving German princes, was laid. From 1804 until 1812, Napoleon successfully expanded the borders of his empire and imposed a continental regime.

During this period, Bonaparte conquered most of Europe. Some territories were coercively annexed and directly administered by France. In other countries, Napoleon established satellite governments that maintained the appearance of autonomy, but in fact, were subjects of the French Empire.

Another category of country maintained its independence through specific treaties signed between their rulers and Napoleon. By 1812, only Portugal, Russia, Sweden, the Kingdom of Sardinia, and Great Britain remained independent and resisted the French onslaught.

The Expansion

In 1804, France annexed Northern Italy and the Swiss Confederation. After the declaration of the empire, Napoleon started his military campaign to conquer more territories. While holding the title of King of Italy, Bonaparte and the French army seized the Low Countries, crossed the Rhine, and captured Vienna in the Third Coalition War, where they faced off against a coalition comprising Austria and Russia.

Then, Napoleon obtained one of his most celebrated triumphs at the battle of Austerlitz. This battle was a landmark in Napoleon's path as an emperor and in his personal career as a strategist and military leader. Therefore, it will be explained in detail in the next chapter.

Prussia (present-day Poland and part of Germany) avoided the invasion and annexation by signing the Treaty of Schönbrunn. According to this treaty, it ceded some territories to France and kept others, but played part of the Napoleonic system in a defensive alliance. Napoleon created the Rhine Confederation and installed a French protectorate. A year later, Napoleon broke this pact and offered one of the principalities to Great Britain, which caused the beginning of the Fourth Coalition War. Prussia allied with Austria and Russia to confront the French Empire.

By 1810, Napoleon eventually found the limits for his expansion, though he ensured his power for the following few years. In 1812, he still had one more ambitious objective in mind: Conquer Russia.

Napoleon's Puppet Governments

The concept of a puppet government refers to a state that claims to be independent but, in fact, is controlled by an external power. It recalls the image of a puppet who moves only because there is a puppeteer moving the strings out of public view (Goddard, n.d.).

Besides controlling the formal territory of the empire, Napoleon had puppet governments in many supposedly independent countries, including Spain, the Grand Duchy of Warsaw, and German kingdoms in Central Europe. These countries preserved their own rulers, but they were nothing but Napoleon's puppets. Some of them were even members of his family (Louis, n.d.).

The first puppet government was installed in the Italian Republic shortly after Napoleon declared himself Emperor and King of Italy. Napoleon appointed his stepson, Eugène de Beauharnais, as viceroy. The formal institutions such as The Consulta and the Legislative Body were preserved, and the constitution wasn't abolished. However, they had no real power over the king's decisions.

This implied that Italian autonomy remained limited, but as Napoleon expanded his domains, it virtually represented an advantage for the Italian kingdom since it constantly increased its territory as compensation (Clark et al., 2023). Originally, the state encompassed the territories of the "former Duchy of Milan, Duchy of Mantua, Duchy of Modena, the western part of the Republic of Venice, part of the Papal States in Romagna, and the province of Novara" (Lumen Learning, n.d., 8). During the following years, Napoleon annexed other principalities and made them the theater of operations against Austria.

Napoleon also attempted to establish a puppet government in Holland and appointed his own brother, Louis Bonaparte, as the king. When he seized power, he tried to ingratiate the people of his new kingdom and said a sentence in poor Dutch. He said *Iek ben Konijn van Olland* which literally means "I'm a rabbit in Holland." He had tried to say, "I'm a 'king' in Holland" (Rijksmuseum, n.d.).

Despite this incident, Louis was sincerely committed to the people of Holland and took his role seriously. Louis was king of Holland between 1806 and 1810 but didn't meet the emperor's expectations. Instead of doing what his brother ordered, he fought for the interests of the Dutch who called him "Louis the Good." The rebel puppet ruler defied his brother's authority, defending the Dutch trade interests and cutting military expenditures, which was disapproved of by Napoleon (De Cleen, 2022).

The French king in Holland was a matter of distress for the emperor and he regretted not putting the country under his direct control. In 1810, he sent French troops to the capital after failing to negotiate with his brother. Louis abdicated and fled his kingdom, and Napoleon annexed Holland to France (Encyclopaedia Britannica, 2023).

Louis wasn't the only brother Napoleon appointed to the throne of a puppet government. He also did so with his older brother, Joseph. First, he named Joseph King of Naples in 1806. Initially, Joseph claimed to be Napoleon's heir when the empire was declared since he didn't have any sons. Napoleon rejected his brother's request and the relationship between them became tense. It worsened when Napoleon appointed Louis to the throne in Holland. Attempting to appease his brother, Napoleon offered him the kingdom of Lombardy, but he refused to accept it.

Later, Napoleon placed Joseph in Naples to remove the Bourbon Dynasty. Instead of following the emperor's instructions, Joseph acted like the real king and enacted several reforms that upset Napoleon. The emperor then decided to take him somewhere else where he could be of use.

In 1807, the French army, led by Napoleon, invaded Spain and pursued the conquest of Portugal. It was the beginning of the Peninsular War. At first, the King of Spain, Charles IV, cooperated as a French ally in an attempt to preserve his kingdoms' autonomy. Nonetheless, Napoleon promoted a palace coup, compelling King Charles to abdicate in favor of his son, Ferdinand VII.

Afterward, Napoleon arranged a meeting with Ferdinand at Bayonne to discuss their alliance. Instead, the Spanish king was arrested and sent to Talleyrand's château. Napoleon appointed his brother Joseph as the new king of the Spanish monarchy and established a puppet government in the Iberian peninsula.

Unfortunately for his ambitions, Napoleon wouldn't succeed in his plan to conquer Portugal, since the Spanish people organized to repel the French invasion. They formed a parallel government through popular assemblies in the main cities and fought guerrilla wars that harassed Napoleon's troops during the Spanish War of Independence. In addition, King Joseph had been forced to flee Madrid in 1808 when the French lost the battle of Baylen. The king was re-established on the throne late that year.

Despite the initial pitfalls, Napoleon conquered most of the peninsula in 1809 (Harrison et al., 2023).

At the same time, other countries that didn't have a puppet government agreed to be satellite states linked by defensive pacts to preserve their autonomy and prevent hostilities. (That was the case of Austria and Prussia, as mentioned above.) Even though they didn't directly respond to the French crown, Napoleon could easily manipulate their governments by threatening military action by France or any of its allied nations. In 1809, the Austrian government, led by Prince Metternich, admitted the impossibility of defeating Napoleon; and, like Prussia, he signed a defensive pact with France.

The Continental System and the Blockade Against Great Britain

During the first year of the empire, Napoleon had only one enemy to fight: Great Britain, the only remaining power from the first two coalitions. By 1803, Napoleon ensured his position on the continent and was ready to venture into an invasion of the British Isles. However, his attempt to attack Great Britain in 1805 failed. The French Grand Army, supported by a Spanish squadron, was defeated in the Battle of Trafalgar by the British fleet commanded by Nelson. This failure dissuaded Napoleon from invading Great

Britain, and, instead, he employed a strategy of economic war: The Continental System.

Napoleon enacted two decrees: Berlin (November 21, 1806) and Milan (December 17, 1807), to proclaim a blockade on British commerce. It implied that France, its allies, and all the neutral countries would not trade with Great Britain. (The alleged neutral countries were, in fact, under French influence.) In sum, almost the whole continent halted commercial relationships with Great Britain.

The main objective was to stifle the British economy, which was going through a process of expansion boosted by the Industrial Revolution. The country had recently lost its colonies in America and depended heavily on the European market. Napoleon's plan was to deprive the British of its most important market and force them to sue for peace. Napoleon argued publicly that the measure was implemented to boost continental Europe's self-sufficiency (Louis, n.d.).

The Continental System was an astute strategy to counteract British naval supremacy. Nevertheless, the outcomes weren't as positive as Napoleon expected. British trade suffered a heavy blow, but it wasn't destroyed. Trading continued through smuggling ports, and many of Napoleon's allies defied the decrees, including his brother Louis, King of Holland, who continued commercial relationships with the island. (This was one of the main reasons why Napoleon sent his troops to overthrow his own brother.) On the other hand, the British also imposed its own blockade on Europe to weaken the French Empire, and, with a stronger navy, it was tighter and more effective.

Relationships with European Monarchs

War and coercive annexation were not the first options considered by Napoleon to expand the empire. Military force was very costly, and Napoleon strategically used it only when other means failed or fell short of accomplishing his goals. Napoleon is perhaps better remembered for his epic battles, but he was also a resourceful politician capable of persuading his rivals to accept his conditions. While fear and the threat of a military invasion were strong disincentives, negotiation and diplomacy were still key elements compelling European leaders to behave in a way that benefited Napoleon.

The defeat at Trafalgar led Napoleon to redirect his strategy and focus on the continent. His successful military campaigns in Europe, earned him an unchallenged authority. From the beginning of the Napoleonic Wars, the European powers formed one coalition after another to limit Napoleon's power. Time after time they failed.

The Third Coalition (Austria and Russia) ended in the French occupation of Vienna, the retirement of the Austrian troops from the Italian principalities that were immediately annexed to France, and the eventual pact signed with Napoleon by Prince Metternich. Austria fought against France in the Third, Fourth, and Fifth Coalition Wars, always at the same cost. Therefore, Metternich proposed that a pact with the French emperor was the only way to keep the monarchy alive.

Napoleon didn't solely rely on military strategies against Austria. He recognized that a strong France posed a threat not only to the Austrian emperor but also to Russia. As a result, Napoleon strategically leveraged Austria's geopolitical position to, if not secure a full alliance, at least reduce the possibility of them becoming an adversary.

Simultaneously, Metternich pursued his own agenda, aiming to establish a new balance of power in Europe where Russia and France could counterbalance each other. However, to achieve this, Central Europe required the strengthening of Prussia and Austria (Kirby et al., 2023).

On the other hand, Prussia had its own trouble. By the beginning of the 19th century, the present-day territories of Poland and Germany consisted of several principalities and the kingdom of Prussia. King Frederick William III of Prussia enacted a foreign policy based on pursuing peace with France and securing an agreement of neutrality. However, Prussia went to war against France with the Fourth Coalition only to experience a catastrophic result. Similar to his actions against Austria, Napoleon used the absolute triumph over Prussia to force a treaty that benefited his empire.

The Treaty of Tilsit (1807) put the Fourth Coalition War to an end after Napoleon defeated the Prussians at Jena and Auerstädt and the Russians at Friedland. However, the consequences weren't identical for both nations. Prussia gave away its territory west of the Elbe River, reducing it to Silesia, Pomerania, Brandenburg, Northwestern Prussia (present-day Poland), and East Prussia. In addition to the occupation of its territory, the king agreed to pay exorbitant sums to the empire.

On the other hand, Russia didn't suffer such negative outcomes. The tsar, Alexander I, had his own aspirations in Central Europe. And, for a while, Napoleon decided to maintain an alliance with him. The Treaty of Tilsit formalized a division of Central and Eastern Europe between the two empires.

The Duchy of Warsaw was created, and Napoleon appointed the allied king of Saxony as the new ruler. He also created the Kingdom of Westphalia in Northern Germany, where his brother Jérôme was assigned as the king. Russia accepted the fragmentation of Prussia, and, in return, Napoleon committed to help the tsar expel the Turks from Russian territories. Eventually, Napoleon saw the weakness of the only big empire that could overshadow his preeminence in the continent. Until 1812, Napoleon played a diplomatic game with his Russian opponent.

The Treaty of Tilsit was the pinnacle of Napoleonic hegemony with the creation of the Grand Empire, which encompassed almost all of continental Europe except for the Balkan states. Napoleon's opponents attempted to use nationalism as a means to incentivize people to rebel against the French invaders. Nonetheless, Napoleon and his effective use of propaganda were more efficient in spreading a new sense of imperial identity.

Chapter Overview

Between 1803 and 18012, Napoleon ensured his power as an emperor within France and reinforced his strategy to expand his domains across Europe. It was the beginning of the Napoleonic Wars. The *Grande Armée* led by Napoleon fought against the consecutive coalitions formed by the other European powers that aimed to stop him. During the period, Napoleon was only defeated in the Battle of Trafalgar by the British navy.

During these years, Napoleon formed the Grand Empire that covered Europe from Portugal to the frontiers of the Russian Empire, from the Low Countries to Italy and the borders of the Ottoman Empire. Many of his conquests were by warfare, but he also masterfully deployed a series of diplomatic and political strategies to gain allies, dissolve potential coalitions against him, and establish puppet governments where he could exercise control without direct rule.

While Napoleon's diplomatic maneuvers painted a grand picture of Europe under his reign, it was on the battlefield that he showcased unparalleled genius. The battle of Austerlitz stands as a testament to this claim.

Chapter 6: Austerlitz— Napoleon's Masterpiece

The battle of Austerlitz is the finest of all I have fought. –Napoleon Bonaparte

Napoleon Bonaparte's military career began in the time of the revolution, and he served in many relevant battles. But what made this battle so significant in Napoleon's eyes, even among all his remarkable military achievements?

The Battle of Austerlitz, also called the Battle of the Three Emperors, took place on December 2, 1805. It was the beginning of the Third Coalition War. The primary cause was "the escalating conflict between Napoleon Bonaparte's French Empire and the Third Coalition, an alliance formed by Russia,

Austria, and several other European powers to oppose French expansion" (History Skills, n.d., para. 6).

The early annexations and the creation of the first puppet governments in the adjacent territories alarmed the European powers. The first two Coalition Wars precipitated the end of the revolutionary government and restored the French monarchy as a Grand Empire. After Napoleon was proclaimed emperor, the Central powers in Europe allied to fight against him and prevent French expansion. Napoleon's response was to lead the *Grande Armeé* to the heart of Central Europe.

By the middle of 1805, Napoleon already occupied Vienna and gained important triumphs against the Austrians and Russians. However, his army was placed in a dangerous position in the environs of Austerlitz (present-day Czech Republic). The enemy surpassed his troops in number, and his soldiers were exhausted. He had to extricate them from danger while keeping them ready to repel a potential attack. He chose Austerlitz to deploy a risky but necessary maneuver.

The Strategy

It wasn't the first time Napoleon faced adverse circumstances. On many other occasions, he managed to engage in combat with an outnumbered army and scarce resources. On the other side, Tsar Alexander I of Russia and Emperor Francis II of Austria led an 86,000-man army. They knew Napoleon's position and aimed to flank him on the right (Simons, 2015).

Napoleon had everything to lose with little margin to effect his troops' retreat without suffering appalling casualties. However, he had developed a genius to leverage the best results, especially with the odds against him. He knew when to show strength and when it was more convenient to feign weakness.

This time, he appeared weak to bait the enemies into a trap. The keys were the terrain and the art of deception that Napoleon had mastered. Napoleon dedicated himself to outlining the perfect plan. There was nothing left to chance. If he was right, and the enemies fell into the trap, it would be an epic victory. If he failed, his men would be at the mercy of the Coalition.

In his book *The Art of War*, the Chinese strategist Sun Tzu emphasized the importance of a military leader's understanding of nature in achieving success in combat. The terrain and the weather conditions played the same important role as the equipment and the professional training of the soldiers (Sun Tzu, n.d.). It is unlikely that Napoleon had read Sun Tzu; but Napoleon's strategy at Austerlitz serves as evidence of the truth of the ancient strategist's advice.

The battlefield was at Pratzen Heights, a hill near the village of Pratze in the region of Moravia. The hill is about 1,000 feet high. According to common sense,

Napoleon, who reached the battlefield first, should have taken the best position: the top of the hill. It was a privileged position because "This high ground separated the area south of the Brunn-Austerlitz road, which was to be Napoleon's main axis of attack, from the villages of Augezd, Tellnitz, and Sokolnitz, which marked the Allies' intended route" (Sigler, n.d., para. 5). Nonetheless, contradicting Sun Tzu's lessons, he decided to resign from that position. Moreover, he would leave one of his divisions to attract the enemy while the majority of his army remained hidden.

The enemy army made the first move. They were operating under Major General Franz von Weyrother's command. They established camp on the east of the hill and started moving during the night of December 1. The columns moved under the command of the Russian General Kutuzov, climbing up the hill. By 8 a.m., the army was coming down the other slope towards Tellnitz in the lower Goldbach valley.

At the bottom of the hill, there were marshes and streams which added obstacles for the battalions to traverse. In the surrounding area, several villages cut across the communication lines between the different divisions of the army, providing opportunities for concealment. All these factors had been thoroughly calculated by Napoleon.

Aware of the weather conditions of the region, Napoleon knew that, early in the morning, a thick fog would work to his benefit, preventing his men from being seen by the enemy. When the Allied army approached, Napoleon launched the first offensive. It was a short and quick movement, and then the French soldiers retreated. The purpose was to provoke the enemy into giving chase.

The Allies acted as expected and followed the retreating French. They had to cross the stream and marshes. Napoleon also knew that during that period of the year, the watery lowlands were covered with an ice sheet. When the Allied soldiers were walking over the marsh, Napoleon ordered artillery to open its bombardment. The ice sheet broke, and hundreds of Austrians and Russians sank into the frozen water.

The Allied army mobilized 40,000 men in its first attack on the French right flank located south of Pratzen Heights. The tsar and the Austrian emperor had fallen into the trap. Napoleon ordered Marshal Davout to resist that first attack. Simultaneously, Napoleon launched another part of the artillery commanded by Marshal Soult:

> "One sharp blow and the war is over," Napoleon told his troops, and at 9 a.m. he ordered his masterstroke — the French troops advanced uphill. As the sun rose and the fog began to lift, the allies watched in horror as the French emerged in force and attacked (Simons, 2015, para. 5).

Then, a corps of 20,000 men attacked the already weakened Allied army enclosed in the center of the Pratzen Plateau. The French, led by Marshal Davout, stormed the Allies and divided their forces. Afterward, the French quickly captured the plateau and Napoleon ordered the final lethal strike (Encyclopaedia Britannica, 2023). At that point, the French had conquered the top of the hill and were placed in the best position to launch the final attack.

One of the French battalions broke the enemy's lines and intensified the attack. Part of the Russian army began to retreat and tried to reach one of the villages. The division under Thiébault's command pursued and intercepted them, captured their guns, and wounded the Russian generals.

The Austro-Russian army was surrounded by the French, which didn't ease up the attack. Eventually, the Allies surrendered. They had suffered about 15,000 casualties, and over 11,000 soldiers were taken prisoner. On the French side, about 9,000 soldiers were dead or wounded. The difference in the number of casualties proves the effectiveness of Napoleon's strategy, even at a disadvantageous starting point. Napoleon's strategy at Austerlitz revolved around deception and exploiting his enemies' mistakes. He deliberately weakened his center, luring the Russians and Austrians into attacking, while maintaining strong flanks.

According to Sigler (2011), Napoleon's strategy at Austerlitz was in line with the key principles of war.

He supported his opinion by analyzing the different moments of the battle.

- **The principle of simplicity:** Napoleon outlined a clear plan with straight orders that avoided misunderstandings, overlapping actions, or hesitation. Every division commander had one direction to follow.
- **The principle of objective:** Each step of the plan had one specific objective. The army was divided into three divisions. Each of them was placed in a certain position on the battlefield and had one purpose.
- **The principle of offensive:** First, seize. Then, retain. Finally, exploit the initiative. One by one, Napoleon's plan included all the steps in the strategy to ensure victory. They first seized the hill, then surrounded and retained the enemy, and finally, pressed until obtaining surrender.
- **The principle of surprise:** Perhaps the decisive one. Napoleon used the surprise factor first, making the enemy believe his center was weak. Then, he allowed the enemy to take the best position on the battlefield to lure them to a trap. Finally, he used weather conditions to hide his soldiers and attack the flanks.
- **The principle of maneuver:** Napoleon reached the battlefield first, which allowed him to

decide where to place the enemy and guide them to the place where he could take advantage of the natural environment.

- **The principle of the economy of forces:** This was a principle often deployed by Napoleon, since he found himself and his army in disadvantageous positions in many other battles. By dividing his troops into divisions, he ensured the best use of the forces he had.

- **The principle of mass:** Napoleon had the guile and wisdom to know when to divide his forces, and he knew the perfect moment for a collective attack with all his troops.

- **The principle of unity of command:** There was one man who knew the strategy, and that was the same man who gave the orders: Napoleon Bonaparte.

Aftermath and the Treaty of Pressburg

Two days later after the Battle of Austerlitz, Francis II of Austria agreed to a suspension of hostilities. He also committed to asking Tsar Alexander I to take his army back to Russia. Napoleon's resounding victory forced Austria's Francis II to conclude the Treaty of Pressburg, ceding Venice to the French kingdom in Italy and temporarily ending the anti-French alliance.

The Battle of Austerlitz brought important changes to the geopolitical landscape in Europe. Napoleon smashed the Russo-Austrian offensive and consolidated his power on the continent. The only remaining enemy was Great Britain. The Russians had no option but to retreat to Poland and the Austrians were forced to sign the Treaty of Pressburg.

The treaty took its name from the city where it was signed: Pressburg (present-day Bratislava, Slovakia). Even though Russia was a member of the coalition and one of the defeated powers, Napoleon focused the punishment of the war on Austria because it was his most direct enemy. The tsar, as explained in the previous chapter, was a potential ally for Napoleon. The French emperor was ready to play a diplomatic card with him and use this power from the East to threaten the nations of Central Europe. Therefore, despite the tsar's participation in the coalition, Napoleon chose to ensure peace and keep the Russian Empire on his side, at least for some time.

Conversely, the treaty weakened the Austrian position, and the Habsburgs lost all their territories in Italy to Napoleon's hands. The victorious campaigns held by Napoleon in 1805 and 1806 allowed him to impose his terms on the defeated Habsburgs. The Austrian monarch and Holy Roman Emperor, Francis II, abdicated his title. Thereafter, he was just Emperor Francis I of Austria. The Austrian monarch held his hostile position against the French Empire for a few years until Prince Metternich drastically changed the Austrian strategy.

Napoleon's army paid a high price, but the Battle of Austerlitz was a turning point in his path to building the Grand Empire. He not only defeated the Coalition but increased his fame across the whole continent: "The treaty was an integral part of Napoleon's policy of creating a ring of French client states beyond the Rhine, the Alps, and the Pyrenees" (Encyclopaedia Britannica, 2022, para. 1).

Napoleon used propaganda as a means to strengthen his power among his people and also to create a favorable image of his power in his enemy's eyes. The triumph at Austerlitz was a major contribution to feeding the idea of his military genius. It would also serve to increase the morale of his troops and reinforce his confidence. The next step would be to advance over the Iberian Peninsula.

In addition to the significant diplomatic achievements enabled by the Treaty of Pressburg, Napoleon had dealt a major blow to the European powers that challenged his supremacy in the continent. The Coalition had failed, and it would take them a long time to recover.

Chapter Overview

Austerlitz wasn't the first or the last battle Napoleon excelled in as a military strategist and leader. However, it was the victory he prized the most. Objectively, it represented the consolidation of his power in Europe, raising a wall around France to restrain any possible advance by the enemies of his empire. The Battle of Austerlitz was proof to himself, and a warning to the rest of the world, of what he was capable of.

As Napoleon stood victorious at Austerlitz, he reached the zenith of his military prowess. Yet, even for a genius, maintaining an empire would bring its own set of unprecedented challenges. In the next chapter, we delve into Napoleon's continuous conflicts, expansive conquests, and the mounting challenges he faced in an ever-shifting European landscape.

Chapter 7: Conflicts, Conquests, and Challenges

During Napoleon's invasion of Russia in 1812, of the more than 600,000 troops in his Grand Army, only around 27,000 returned to France. This disastrous campaign resulted in one of the most catastrophic military retreats in history, starkly illustrating the dangers of overextension and the severe Russian winter (Greenspan, 2023). But what led to the disaster?

One of the greatest challenges Napoleon had to face was the resistance of the Spanish population when the French troops invaded the Iberian Peninsula. Despite Napoleon's talent for capitalizing on pitfalls, learning lessons, and reshaping his strategies, the Spanish resisted with British support. For the first time, the French were pushed back into their territories.

Between 1809 and 1810, Napoleon consolidated his power, and the empire reached its largest extent. He had ensured internal peace and personal power. Through the Continental System based on dominance and alliances there wasn't any country that could challenge him. The whole continent was virtually at war with Great Britain, the only remaining enemy, and the Russian Empire was a distant ally. Even so, Napoleon made the daring decision to invade Russia. Why would Napoleon risk all he had accomplished?

It is fair to wonder how power can be continuously rejuvenated if there isn't any conflict to deal with. Napoleon's ascent to power was framed by the chaos unleashed by the revolution. The birth of the empire happened in the heat of an external war against Europe. The threat of a foreign invasion enabled the mobilization of thousands of citizens inspired by a new sense of nationalism, who marched to war to defend their emperor. Was it possible to sustain such a large and complex empire in peace and stability?

Napoleon must have considered Russia a permanent potential enemy since the tsar had his own expansionist intentions. A weak Central Europe was certainly an invitation for the Russians to advance. It is hard to calculate which was a greater risk for Napoleon: To keep the unstable alliance with another ambitious leader or to gamble his army in one of the most monumental military campaigns in the history of warfare. He decided on the latter.

The Peninsular War: New Tactics and Lessons

Napoleon's struggle in the Iberian Peninsula contributed considerably to his eventual downfall. However, the outcomes weren't completely negative at the beginning. Until 1813 the conflict in Spain and Portugal, though costly, served Napoleon's interests in Central and Eastern Europe. However, the actions in Spain had an indirect effect on the progress of French affairs in the east.

Napoleon invaded Spain in 1807 with a plan in mind to reach Portugal, Great Britain's major ally on the continent. By means of diplomatic devices, Napoleon arranged the abdication of King Charles I and, later, of his heir, Ferdinand VII, in favor of the French emperor's brother, Joseph Bonaparte. After repelling social upheaval from the Spanish people who rebelled against the invaders, Joseph settled in Madrid as the new king.

However, the Spanish actions to restore their own king didn't stop. Instead, it evolved into a guerrilla war that forced Napoleon to come up with innovative strategies and techniques. Great Britain engaged in the conflict as it offered an opportunity to confront French power in the continent. It was called the Peninsular War, and it was fought between 1808 and 1814. The British army joined its forces with the Spanish resistance and the Portuguese troops. Together, they carried the war to France and took the first step toward Napoleon's overthrow.

After the Battle of Bayleen, the French emperor ensured his position in Spain. However, the Spanish sought British help. In August 1808, a force of 14,000 British soldiers landed at Montego Bay in Portugal. While the British army obtained the first important victories over the French, the Spanish played a key role in defending and recovering control in the cities

and villages. This war interested the British in particular because it represented the only important
contribution to opposing Napoleon's progress on the
continent between 1793 and 1814. All the other British interventions in the Coalition Wars had ended in
failure.

The French forces were embedded in a type of
war they didn't know how to fight:

> French troops were also required to garrison
> hostile territory and wage a bitter war against
> Spanish and Portuguese insurgents, the 'guer-
> rillas'. French communications and supply lines
> were harassed by their raids and ambushes. By
> 1812, the French had over 350,000 soldiers in
> Iberia, but 200,000 were protecting lines of
> supply rather than serving as front-line troops
> (National Army Museum, n.d., para. 12).

The Spanish rebels and the Portuguese forces
fought courageously in the cities of Oporto, Almeida,
Cadiz, Badajoz, and Salamanca, among others. In
1812, the situation for the French in the peninsula
worsened since Napoleon ordered a large part of the
army to withdraw and go back to France. They had a
new target in the east. He had decided to invade Russia, and he needed the bulk of his army for the new
military campaign.

With decimated forces, the French attempted to
hold their position in Spain. However, on June 21, the
British army led a massive attack on Victoria. The
battle resulted in a catastrophe for the French, since

about 5,000 soldiers were killed and 3,000 were taken as war prisoners, but Joseph Bonaparte had time to escape. It was the end of the French occupation of the peninsula and also a sign for the Austrians and the other powers to rejoin and create a new coalition to go against Napoleon (National Army Museum, n.d.).

The Invasion of Russia

Napoleon had many reasons to go to Russia. Even though Tsar Alexander I became an ally after the Treaty of Tilsit, Napoleon was not ignorant of Russian interests in Europe and the Balkan Peninsula. A Russian operation to expand Alexander's empire was only a matter of time. Napoleon also hoped to compel Tsar Alexander I of Russia to cease trading with British merchants through proxies, in an effort to pressure the United Kingdom to sue for peace. The official political aim of the campaign was to liberate Poland from the threat of Russia.

These circumstances persuaded Napoleon to bring back a major part of his army from Spain to lead a military campaign to invade the vast territories of Russia. It is usually heard that Napoleon made a huge mistake by neglecting the weather conditions and that, eventually, it was the Russian winter that defeated him. Indeed, winter played a key role in his failed campaign, but it wasn't a problem of neglect or miscalculation. Even the best plans can be hampered by imponderables. On the other hand, the Russians also used their scarce resources efficiently.

As he always did, Napoleon had a thorough plan to invade Russia. He calculated the men, supplies, and conditions of the terrain to ensure access to what his troops needed. He outlined a map with roads and villages that could take men, weapons, and goods. He planned a campaign that would last 30 days at the most, and by the arrival of the winter, they would have already conquered Moscow.

For this campaign, Napoleon gathered the largest army that had ever existed in Europe. He led the troops and equipment to Neman, and on June 24, 1812, they crossed the river to enter Russian territory. The *Grande Armée* encompassed 453,000 soldiers among which were about 200,000 French. The rest came from the occupied nations or the allied kingdoms (Encyclopaedia Britannica, 2023).

Even though there were no direct engagements, conditions were far worse than Napoleon imagined. The terrain was severely challenging, impeding their progress, and the supply lines proved inefficient. This resulted in supplies failing to adequately support the troops, consequently weakening the infantry. Meanwhile, the cavalry, a key element in Napoleon's strategy, was seriously hampered. The excessive work, hunger, and disease resulted in the death of many horses.

> History has taught us that Napoleon, in his invasion of Russia in 1812, marched into Moscow with his army largely intact and retreated only because the citizens of Moscow burned three-fourths of the city, depriving the army of food and supplies. The harsh Russian winter then devastated the army as it retreated (Knight, 2012, para. 1).

However, there was another unexpected, silent enemy that wreaked havoc among the French troops: typhus. The tough conditions of the Russian territory and the endemic disease caused considerable losses to Napoleon even on his way toward Moscow.

As the French marched, they didn't find major opposition from the Russians. The most significant combat was near Moscow. The French confronted the

Russian army, who had taken a position in a small town called Borodino, 70 miles west of Moscow. "The battle that followed was the largest and bloodiest single-day action of the Napoleonic Wars, involving more than 250,000 soldiers and resulting in 70,000 casualties" (*Invasion of Russia*, n.d., 7). On September 17 (two months later than Napoleon's initial schedule), Napoleon and a 95,000-man army entered Moscow. That night, the city was on fire. The Russians themselves set it.

Winter was close, and it was too risky to attempt to survive among the ruins of the city. Napoleon ordered his men to withdraw. By then, the *Grande Armée* consisted of 110,000 men. They left Moscow on October 19 in excellent condition. By November, the forces had dropped to 55,000 men.

The Russians implemented the technique of scorched earth. Instead of engaging in battles, the Russian army destroyed villages, crops, and roads. As the French advanced, they found no supplies to survive on. Soon, winter came and found them weak and starved. Then, the Russians pursued them and fought against them.

The aftermath of the invasion was terrible. From about 612,000 combatants only 112,000 returned to the borders of the French empire. About 100,000 were killed in action, mainly in the first battle before reaching Moscow. A further 200,000 died from other causes, including typhus and hunger. 50,000 were abandoned in hospitals, 50,000 deserted, and

100,000 were taken as prisoners of war (Encyclopaedia Britannica, 2023). The Russians suffered about 400,000 casualties and were left with a devastated country. That was the high price they paid to save their nation from invasion.

The failed campaign to Russia was a resounding blow to Napoleon's power. It took the war to Russia, allowing European powers to regroup and prepare a new offensive. If Austerlitz had given Napoleon outstanding fame as a military genius, the disastrous campaign to Russia had the opposite effect. His enemies stopped considering him invincible, and his men were demoralized.

The Battle of Leipzig

Also called the Battle of the Nations, the Battle of Leipzig was fought between October 16–19, 1813. It ended in the decisive defeat of Napoleon. This forced him to retreat from Poland and Germany.

On one front, the fatigued *Grande Armée*, under the leadership of Napoleon, had recently commenced its retreat following the Russian campaign. On the opposing front, a fresh coalition emerged, uniting all the nations that had become adversaries during Napoleon's years in power. Troops from Austria, Prussia, Russia, and Sweden came together to face the French army. They were respectively commanded by Prince Karl Philipp Schwarzenberg, General

Gebhard Leberecht Blücher, General Leonty Leontyevich Bennigsen, and the Swedish crown prince Jean Bernadotte.

The battle took place at Leipzig, in Saxony. The *Grande Armée* had about 185,000 soldiers. The Allied troops had about 320,000. With more than 90,000 casualties, it was one of the biggest and bloodiest battles in European history (Encyclopaedia Britannica, 2023).

After the withdrawal of his troops from Russia in 1812, Napoleon moved his operations center to Germany. Here, he attempted a new offensive to destroy the army of Bohemia in 1813. Nonetheless, he failed to take Berlin and continued his retreat until reaching the banks of the Elbe River.

The coalition approached and threatened French communication lines. Napoleon decided to settle in Leipzig. On October 16, he made his next move and

"successfully thwarted the attacks of Schwarzenberg's 78,000 men from the south and Blücher's
54,000 men from the north, but he failed to defeat
either decisively. The number of troops surrounding
him increased during the lull on the 17th" (Encyclopaedia Britannica, 2023, para. 1).

The Battle Day by Day

October 16th: The Opening Moves. The battle commenced in the early morning, with a
promising start for Napoleon. As in previous encoun-
ters, he divided his forces to coordinate the assault.
Initially, he commanded an intense cannonade
aimed at immobilizing the Russian troops between
the village and the hills. Despite being outnumbered,
the French held a strategically advantageous position
on the battlefield. Nevertheless, unlike the situation
at Austerlitz, Napoleon was unable to launch the final
assault in a timely manner. This delay allowed an Allied division to breach the enemy's defensive line, as
another Allied division had managed to halt their
progress from the north.

Napoleon had to wait until 2 p.m. to have "the
decisive moment," as he called it, to make the key
move. Then, all the divisions launched the final attack. However, this time, the enemy also had
reinforcements. In the evening, when the fire of artillery stopped, the positions were much the same, but

the Allies were expecting 100,000 fresh soldiers to reinforce their position.

October 17: A Pause. Both armies took time to rest and wait for reinforcements. Napoleon should have understood that he was in a disadvantageous position and decided to withdraw. Instead, he attempted a strategy that had worked well in the past.

October 18: The Betrayal. The fight started in the morning, but this time, all the Allied forces launched a simultaneous attack on Napoleon's army. In the middle of the battle, Napoleon's allied contingent from Saxony and the cavalry from Wurtemberg unexpectedly changed sides and started fighting against the French. Even in this situation, Napoleon was determined to keep fighting. The coalition had almost 320,000 soldiers against only 170,000 French men resisting as they could. However, the French ended the day without surrender.

October 19: The Final Blow. The fight continued, and Napoleon had no choice but to retreat. He gave the order to his men, but when they tried to withdraw through the single bridge over the Elster River, the Allied forces destroyed it, and the French soldiers found themselves in a trap. About 30,000 of them were captured. The total aftermath was terrible, with about 100,000 French men killed or wounded, against 54,000 for the Allies (*1813 and the Lead-up to the Battle of Leipzig*, 2013).

The Battle of Leipzig is considered the turning point in the Napoleonic Wars. The French defeat was the beginning of the end of the Napoleonic Empire.

Forced to abandon his plan to conquer all of Europe, Napoleon was at the mercy of the Coalition. In 1814, the Allied forces reached the capital of the empire and Napoleon was forced to abdicate. Afterward, he was exiled to the isle of Elba.

After Napoleon's defeat, European powers outlined a new European order. The so-called Congress of Vienna, signed the Final Act on June 9, 1815, established a new balance of power by redrawing the political map. The purpose was to never allow any nation to be powerful enough to attempt an imperial expansion and to strengthen Central European kingdoms to inhibit any imperialist ambition from greater powers. The system ensured peace for more than 50 years.

Chapter Overview

Napoleon reached the pinnacle of his career within a considerably short time. His failed invasion of Russia and the Battle of Leipzig were irreversible turning points for him. This invites us to reflect:

- Why was the Battle of Leipzig significant in the coalition's resistance against Napoleon?
- How did Napoleon's previous decisions impact the outcome of this battle?
- How did the shifting alliances among European powers during this period influence the outcome of the Battle of Leipzig?

- In what ways did Napoleon's military strategies at Leipzig differ from his previous battles, and how might this have affected the battle's outcome?
- Considering the vast number of troops and the diversity of the Coalition forces, what logistical challenges might have affected both sides during the Battle of Leipzig?
- How was the morale of Napoleon's *Grande Armee* compared to that of the Coalition forces, and how might morale have influenced the battle's result?
- Beyond the immediate military implications, how did the Battle of Leipzig reshape political and territorial arrangements in Europe?

Napoleon, once Europe's indomitable conqueror, was now facing consequences for his overreach. As alliances formed against him, the stage was set for one final, iconic battle that would decide his fate and reshape Europe's future.

Chapter 8: Waterloo—The End of an Era

Waterloo was not just a defeat on the battlefield; it was the crumbling of an empire and the end of an era in Europe. Even though Liepzieg ended the Napoleonic Empire, it wasn't the definitive end of his time in power. He still had one more battle to fight.

Napoleon would prove that even though he was away from France and deprived of most of his resources, he was still powerful. The world had changed because of him, and he would find a way back. Nonetheless, it would only last long enough to add a new page to history under his name.

After Leipzig, the Senate of France forced Napoleon I to abdicate in favor of his son, Napoleon II. Nevertheless, the Royalists were determined to get rid of the emperor and compelled his son to abdicate. The Bourbon Dynasty was restored to the throne, and Napoleon was exiled to the Island of Elba as a consequence of his defeat at Leipzig.

However, removing Napoleon from the throne wasn't enough to tear down the power he built for almost 20 years. Throughout all those years, he devoted himself to expanding the French frontiers and increasing his power through warfare and diplomatic relationships. He had been wise enough to create a strong foundation for his power: the people's loyalty and love.

Similar to many political leaders, Napoleon faced significant opposition both within his realm and beyond. His critics accused him of behaving despotically, while others asserted nationalist motives in their resistance against French invasions and oppression. Furthermore, many individuals were primarily motivated by personal ambitions for power.

Conversely, Napoleon also garnered substantial support. His followers viewed him as the figure who restored order and upheld the ideals of the revolution. To them, Napoleon was a national hero, dedicated to advancing the greatness of his country, and they ardently desired his return to power.

Cent Jours—The Hundred Days

Napoleon was 45 years old when he arrived on the Island of Elba on April 20, 1814. He was appointed as the ruler of the island, which had about 12,000 inhabitants. The treaty he had signed with the winning powers allowed him to be called "Emperor."

Yet, he was a prisoner. He was under constant Austrian and French guard. Even though he seemed to be pleased with his new life, he still received letters and newspapers from France. Somehow, he learned that many people still supported him there.

On February 26, 1815, Napoleon found a way to evade his guards and escaped from the island. He even passed an English ship without being noticed, and shortly after landed in France. There, he gathered an army that was already waiting for him. His comeback had been organized by conspirators in France. His followers continued to work and wait for Napoleon's return:

> During the first few months of Louis XVIII's reign, the violet became the rallying emblem for Bonapartists. This discreet spring flower was seen as a symbol of loyalty to Napoleon and indicated a hope that a Bonaparte would return to the throne (Timeline: Consulate/1st French Empire, n.d., para. 59).

The news of his comeback spread like wildfire, and "Immediately, people and troops began to rally to the returned Emperor. French police forces were sent to arrest him, but upon arriving in his presence, they kneeled before him" (SparkNotes, n.d., para. 2). This peaceful sign of respect to the formerly-abdicated Napoleon told him everything he needed to know about the loyalty of the French people.

When he was approaching Paris, the royal guard intercepted him. Napoleon ordered his men to wait and not to attack. Instead, he walked alone towards the guard and said in a loud voice: "Soldiers, if there is one among you who wants to kill his general, his Emperor, here I am." (*Napoleon at War*, n.d., para. 3) He opened his coat and showed his chest as if he was ready to be shot. None of the men fired—instead, all of them cheered "Long live the Emperor." His glory hadn't been forgotten by the soldiers he led so many times before.

He had a triumphant entrance to the city that had once surrendered to his feet on March 20, 1815. Paris welcomed him and people celebrated his return. The recently appointed king, Louis XVIII, didn't know how to handle the situation and fled to Belgium. Without any loss of time, Napoleon I occupied the Palace of the Tuileries and claimed his crown as an emperor. It was the beginning of the period known as "Cent Jours" (The Hundred Days).

During this time, Napoleon tried to implement reforms to gain popular support which declined as the days passed. The enthusiasm for the emperor's comeback had become diluted. Meanwhile, Louis XVIII and the Bourbon Royalists hurried to organize an offensive to prevent Napoleon from restoring his power.

Napoleon knew his enemies wouldn't take long to act against him, so he decided to make the first move. He invaded Belgium with an army of 130,000 men and defeated the Prussians. Then, he prepared for the next battle, which would take place at Waterloo, south of Brussels.

The Last Battle

After Napoleon's arrival in Paris, Austria, Prussia, Great Britain, and Russia agreed to maintain a force of 150,000 men near the border until he was overthrown. When Napoleon invaded Belgium, they increased the number to 794,000. Meanwhile, Russian troops advanced to the Rhine.

On the other side, Napoleon had 160,000 men, but he had to assign part of this force to the frontiers. Louis XVIII abolished conscription, a resource Napoleon had used to increase the size of his *Grande Armée* in the past. Even so, he gathered 80,000 men to add to his troops within the 100 days he was on the throne. By June of 1815, his army had 500,000 men, but they didn't reach him in time to assist at Waterloo (Encyclopaedia Britannica, 2023).

Napoleon's campaign started in April of 1815, when he decided to attack Wellington and Blücher, British and Prussian generals, in the southern Netherlands. After the first French victory, the Allied forces regrouped and prepared for a new offensive. Napoleon turned his attention to the British army, led by the Duke of Wellington. They had taken a defensive position at the top of a hill near Waterloo. Despite the similarity in forces, the French army was formed by experienced professional soldiers, while the British were mainly conscripts who had never been in combat. Wellington depended upon the arrival of the Prussian army that was on their way to back them.

On the morning of June 18, Napoleon was ready to attack. The position and conditions were similar to many other battles. However, that morning there was a heavy rain, and he had to wait hours to launch his first attack. The terrain was muddy, and it hampered the advance of his troops. That was a costly mistake. Those hours were decisive because they gave Wellington time to wait for reinforcements, whereas Napoleon thought the rain would delay the arrival of more enemy armies.

During the first hours of the battle, Napoleon attempted to deploy his proven strategies of dividing his troops, surrounding the enemy, and breaking his lines. As the battle raged on at Waterloo, Napoleon became increasingly confident of victory. The British and their allies were on the brink of collapse under the relentless assault of the French. However, in the afternoon, the distant boom of cannons from the east signaled a new development. The Prussians, led by Blücher, had evaded the French troops meant to delay them and were approaching.

Napoleon's traditional strategies were useless this time. The British soldiers fought bravely and resisted more than expected. Later, the arrival of the Prussian army tipped the balance in favor of the coalition. Napoleon miscalculated the time it would take him to control the battlefield and launch the final attack on the British. When the Prussians arrived, they broke Napoleon's army's lines, and it was too late for a counterattack.

Napoleon, now realizing the impending danger, dispatched a significant part of his army to hold off the Prussians. This division of forces weakened his main assault against the British and their allies. The Prussian army, though exhausted from their prior engagements, attacked with vigor. Their dramatic arrival and the pressure they exerted on Napoleon's eastern flank changed the battle's dynamics.

The French army was suddenly outnumbered and surrounded. Their enemies attacked on both flanks, and they separated, trying to repel the cavalry advances. Napoleon had to admit that the battle was lost and ordered his men to retreat.

As the French soldiers withdrew, the British and the Prussians pursued them. The emperor escaped, but many of his men were killed or wounded, and others were captured as prisoners. It was the end, not only of the battle, but of Napoleon's dream of rebuilding his empire.

The battle left a horrible number of 25,000 French men killed on the battlefield, and about 9,000 captured. It was also a high price that the European powers paid to prevent Napoleon's return to power. Wellington's troops suffered 15,000 casualties and Blücher's allies nearly 8,000 (Encyclopaedia Britannica, 2023).

After the victory, the Duke of Wellington said: "My heart is broken by the terrible loss I have sustained in my old friends and companions and my poor soldiers. Believe me, nothing except a battle lost can be half so melancholy as a battle won" (Libquotes.com, nd.).

After leaving the battlefield, Napoleon came back to Paris. Defeated, he had no choice but to abdicate the following morning. His troops marched to the Loire River and were later dismissed. The Allies entered Paris and restored Louis XVIII to the throne. Napoleon was taken prisoner by the British.

Downfall at St. Helena

After the defeat at Waterloo, Napoleon fled to the island of Aix. From there he wanted to travel to the United States. Meanwhile, the French and other European powers wanted to make sure he could never escape and return again, so this time they took stricter security measures. However, Napoleon didn't fight against them anymore. Instead, he surrendered unconditionally to the British who had captured him.

The captors hesitated to return the prisoner to the French king for punishment, doubting its efficacy. The British were skeptical about Louis' ability to make the correct decision. Elba had already proven ineffective in detaining Bonaparte from Europe. The British knew of Napoleon's intentions to go to America and were resolute in thwarting them. Consequently, a choice was made to confine him to a remote island in the Atlantic Ocean, known as St. Helena. There were two primary reasons for this decision:

> first because of a desire not to keep Napoleon in England or even in Europe, for fear that he would become the object of public curiosity, and perhaps ultimately of compassion, but

above all due to the fear that he might once again be the source of a revolutionary uprising (Boudon, n.d., para. 7).

After a two-month journey, Napoleon and a small entourage landed on the small island surrounded by high cliffs and the agitated waters of the ocean. It was impossible to escape from there; it was a natural prison. Longwood, his new residence, was a barn with wet and dark rooms. The environment and the weather conditions quickly affected Napoleon's health, even though his food was good, and he was allowed to move freely about the island.

Chapter Overview

After being defeated at Leipzig, Napoleon was forced to abdicate and leave the palace. At noon on April 20, 1814, he met his guard when he was departing. All the soldiers were in respectful silence and then, he spoke to them:

> Soldiers of my Old Guard, I bid you farewell. For twenty years you have been my constant companions on the road to honor and glory. In these latter times, as in the days of our prosperity, you have never ceased to be models of courage and fidelity. With men such as you, our cause would not have been lost; but the war would have been interminable; [...] Do not lament my fate; the only reason I have allowed

myself to survive was so that I could further
serve our glory (Napoleon's adieux to the Old
Guard at Fontainebleau, 20 April, 1814, n.d.,
para. 2).

Then, a subordinate approached and gave him
the standard. Napoleon kissed him as a symbol of
gratitude and respect for the men who had served
him. The soldiers sobbed and remained in silence.
For many French, Napoleon was a hero, a fighter for
their national pride. That enabled him to have a successful comeback from Elba.

But many other French people and the rest of the
European powers had a vivid, and not so fond,
memory of what Napoleon, with his talent and his
ambition, could do. Therefore, there were no delays
in launching a massive attack. Waterloo was the end,
but they still had to ensure he had no options to attempt to seize power again. Therefore, he had to be
taken to the end of the world, the island of St. Helena.
There, he would spend his last years.

As the winds of Waterloo settle and Napoleon
finds himself isolated on the remote island of St. Helena, we transition from the grand stages of
battlefields to the intimate corridors of Napoleon's
personal life. The man who once controlled vast territories now reflects on his relationships, health, and
the life that is slipping away.

Chapter 9: Personal Life, Relationships, and Health

Using his family to ensure power and avoid problems didn't always work as expected for Napoleon. Joseph was reluctant to adopt his brother's strategies and was moved by his own ambitions. He wasn't comfortable running a puppet government in Naples. Then, Joseph proved to be unable to control the situation with the rebels in Spain which eventually led to the Peninsular War.

Joseph wasn't the only brother who failed Napoleon. Louis didn't understand his role as a puppet ruler and instead assumed his role as the real King of Holland. While this was good for the kingdom and the people of Holland, it worked against Napoleon's interests. Louis hampered the blockade against Great Britain and inadvertently helped them maintain their influence on the continent.

Marriages, Affairs, and Children

Love and politics are a rare combination. Marriages and love affairs were usually subordinated to political interests in the times of Napoleon. However, he was a passionate man, not only in defense of his ideas and pursuit of political power, but also in his intimate life. For him, love, a personal life, and the concerns of the state were inextricably linked. This doesn't necessarily mean, however, that any of his sentimental choices weren't guided by other, less emotional factors.

Napoleon married twice, first to Josephine, Viscountess of Beauharnais, and then, to Marie Louise, Duchess of Parma. While the second marriage was strongly linked to diplomatic and political interests, Napoleon's romance and marriage with Josephine seems to have been founded in love – to which the passionate letters they exchanged bear witness.

Napoleon was 26 years old when he met Josephine at a gathering at Paul Barras' place. Barras was the Governor of France and Napoleon's mentor. Josephine was 32 years old, and a widow. Her first husband had been executed during The Terror. However, he and Josephine had already been separated.

Josephine wasn't her real name, but it was what Napoleon called her. Her full name was Marie-Josèphe Rose de Tascher de la Pagerie, and she belonged to an impoverished aristocratic family. She had two daughters from her marriage, and when Napoleon met her, she was Barras' mistress. At first blush, there are few signs this was a political relationship between Napoleon and Josephine. When they met in 1795, Napoleon was just at the beginning of his military career. It could have been genuine love.

Napoleon and Josephine got married in March 1796, just when he appeared as a promising prospect in the convulsive political environment of Paris. Only four days after the wedding, Napoleon interrupted his honeymoon to march on Italy and lead his first important military mission. It is believed that Napoleon feared Josephine's infidelities, but he cared sincerely for her and her children (NGV, nd.).

When he seized power, he found prominent positions for his stepchildren: "Hortense, married Napoleon's brother Louis, who became King of Holland and Eugène became Bonaparte's loyal deputy and later French Prince, Prince of Venice and Viceroy of Italy, among other titles" (NGV, n.d., para. 10).

After Italy, Napoleon was kept away from his family for more time during his campaign to Egypt. While her husband was away, Josephine bought Malmaison, a palace outside Paris. She made it a beautiful place, with carefully designed and cultivated gardens.

On December 2, 1804, after crowning himself emperor, Napoleon crowned Josephine as the Empress of France. She played important official roles and was a significant support for Bonaparte in daily court issues. However, she failed on one major objective: She couldn't give him an heir, the key to discouraging assassination attempts.

In 1810, Josephine's marriage with Napoleon was annulled. At first, Josephine was upset, but in the end, they reached good terms. Napoleon allowed her to keep the title of empress and to live in their palace of Malmaison.

Napoleon was deeply concerned about his lack of an heir. He had been searching for a new wife even before divorcing Josephine. The Emperor of France needed a woman who could give him a son and perhaps some strategic political alliances.

Napoleon chose Marie Louise of the House of Habsburg. She was the youngest child of the Austrian emperor, Francis I, and grandniece of Marie Antoinette. Initially, Napoleon wanted to marry Grand Duchess Anna, daughter of Tsar Paul I of Russia, but it caused alarm in Austria. Prince Metternich, who was trying to improve diplomatic relationships between his country and France, suggested Marie Louise. That marriage sealed the alliance between France and Austria.

The wedding was quickly arranged and took place in Vienna on March 11, 1810. Marie Louise was 19 years old, and she didn't meet her 40-year-old fiancé until after the wedding; the groom wasn't at the ceremony. In his place, the bride's uncle, Archduke Charles, stood on behalf of the emperor.

Despite the first impression, Marie Louise developed tender feelings for Napoleon, as she told her father in a letter: "'He loves me very much. I respond to his love sincerely. There is something very fetching and very eager about him that is impossible to resist'" (Rouget, n.d., para 5).

While Josephine was an active member of the court even after the divorce, Marie Louise was shy and withdrawn and didn't interfere in political affairs. Napoleon continued his relationship with Josephine as a friend and counselor, though he didn't approve of her many romantic affairs and wasteful life. Instead, he prized Marie Louise's prudence and modesty.

Finally, on March 20, 1811, Marie Louise fulfilled the emperor's greatest expectations. She gave birth to Napoleon's child, and it was a boy, the French heir. His name was Napoléon François Joseph Charles Bonaparte. He was given the title King of Rome, following the tradition of the Holy Roman Empire.

In 1813, while Napoleon was at war against Germany, Marie Louise was appointed Regent, although it was merely a *de jure* position and Napoleon made all the decisions. She wrote constantly to her husband on the battlefront, informing him of the situation in

Paris, and she also attempted to earn her father's support for Napoleon, but she didn't succeed. Austria joined the alliance against the emperor.

When the Allies approached Paris in 1814 after defeating Napoleon at Leipzig, Marie Louise refused to leave her palace. She was the daughter of the Austrian emperor and she believed she should be treated with respect. She eventually left, but she didn't expect her husband would be dethroned.

Napoleon was compelled to abdicate, but he was allowed to appoint his wife to the duchies of Parma, Piacenza, and Guastalla, naming her son as heir. Marie Louise was advised not to join him on Elba. She accepted the arrangement but kept her loyalty to her husband.

When Napoleon was defeated at Waterloo, Marie Louise didn't join him. She also stopped writing to him. The Congress of Vienna officialized her titles in Piacenza, Parma, and Guastalla, but forbade her son to son to inherit them.

Health Concerns

The health concerns of rulers are (perhaps) far more important than intimate issues; they are a matter of the state because they can trigger internal and external conflicts. They can encourage conspiracies, weaken institutions, or invite external forces to take action against the country. This is a strong reason to keep a rulers' health shrouded in secrecy as much as possible. Napoleon wasn't an exception to this rule, and therefore, there have been several speculations on his health and the causes of his death at St. Helena.

One of Napoleon's health concerns that has excited interest is his alleged epilepsy. Several scholars have pointed out that there is evidence to prove Napoleon had seizures (Hughes, 2003; Andrews, 1895). It is hard to know if the physicians of the court gave the seizures that name, but there are several testimonies of attacks the emperor suffered (Andrews, 1895). It is also affirmed that his "psychogenic attacks were likely related to the tremendous stress in his life and the epileptic seizures were the result of chronic uremia from a severe urethral stricture caused by gonorrhea that was transmitted from his wife, Empress Josephine" (Hughes, 2003, para. 1).

According to records, Napoleon's health started to decline when he reached the age of 40. Before the battle of Borodino, during the invasion of Russia, he was infected with a severe cold which triggered dysuria. Despite his physician's advice to delegate the command, Napoleon never admitted to being weak and continued with his endeavors. This might have led him to make poor decisions during that mission (Niderost, 2022).

He also suffered stomach issues. Some of the most relevant episodes happened during the battles of Dresden and Leipzig. The time when his health declined coincides with the period when his military endeavors lost some of his brilliance:

> As Napoleon's health declined, so did his decision-making abilities, although he was still capable of real brilliance in planning and executing a campaign. But after 1810 there were more and more moments of indecision, of hesitation, than had been seen in earlier years (Niderost, 2022, para. 6).

His bad health might have impacted his decision to attack the Russians with a frontal movement instead of choosing the flanks. That led him to a bloody battle with long-term consequences, preventing him from achieving his goal. Also, he suffered from terrible stomach pains during the battle of Leipzig and before Waterloo, when he and his army were preparing for the attack on the British forces.

Then, his health worsened when he was confined to the island of St. Helena. Due to either the climate or the passivity of his life there, Napoleon became ill. Even though many speculated he could have been poisoned, evidence indicates he suffered from stomach cancer (Spary, 2022) or ulcers. The reports signed just after Napoleon's autopsy on May 6 by British doctors and Francesco Antommarchi show strong medical evidence for this final diagnosis as the cause of death: "advanced malignant gastric neoplasia associated with upper gastrointestinal bleeding" (Lugli et al., 2021, para. 19).

Chapter Overview

Behind the bronze statues and the legend of the great emperor, there was a man who was a son, brother, husband, and father. He dealt with the complex political affairs of his nation while juggling the same sentimental and health issues as any other mortal.

His family played a key role in his formative years, and even more during his process of building an empire. Love and politics were central to his life, and despite the pragmatism that led to most of his actions, he didn't neglect the love and affection of either of his wives.

Even though he was strong and considered himself a man made for work, his body was vulnerable. It is impossible to guess how events would have evolved if his body hadn't deteriorated.

Having explored the personal life of Napoleon, a man of immense influence and complexity, we must now address a question that has intrigued historians for centuries: Was Napoleon a hero who championed the ideals of the French Revolution, or was he a tyrant who sought only personal power and glory?

Chapter 10: The Duality of Napoleon—Hero or Tyrant?

Napoleon Bonaparte: A name that simultaneously evokes admiration and controversy. Was he a visionary leader or a ruthless tyrant?

Human nature tends to judge. There is a natural desire to separate the good from the bad, the virtuous from the flawed, the hero from the villain. With historical figures like Napoleon, such judgment and classification is almost impossible. Perhaps, historical knowledge and the analysis of the past don't provide elements for a trial, but only an education. It is pointless to attempt to demonize or glorify his name. It is enough to highlight all he did that earned him a privileged place in history, and what the world should be aware of if any other figure like him should rise again.

Whenever a historical character is scrutinized, the context must always be a frame of reference. People owe much to the social and cultural processes that shape their lives, their interests, and their options. Some people, like Napoleon, live their lives within those frames; but they also transform them. Napoleon wasn't only a son of his era but also the father of the following one. For good or ill, his actions shaped the contemporary world.

There are moments in history when the whole social structure shakes. Most people are carried away by bewilderment, chaos, and fear. Only a few can see through the dust and shadows of a deep crisis. They can be blamed for taking advantage of the circumstances, or they can be cherished for building a new world from the ashes.

Napoleon's name towered among the ruins of a society that claimed modernization, equality, and justice, and later submerged in an endless spiral of violence. Napoleon was capable of understanding people's discontent and inspiring new revolutionary and nationalist sentiments that would gain massive support and take French ideals to the rest of Europe. This inaugurated an era of wars that extended violence outside the French frontiers. Napoleon sowed the seeds of battle across Europe for almost 15 years and originated a new system of international law, recalibrating diplomatic relationships among the countries.

Napoleon built as much as he destroyed. He worked for the greatness of France, and he used his nation to enhance his personal glory. There are always two sides to history. Sometimes, the best thing to do is highlight the controversies and let the angel and the demon coexist.

Positive Reforms Versus Autocratic Rule

One of the most significant aspects of Napoleon's life was his political career. Boosted by the French Revolution, Napoleon passed from being a Corsican nationalist to a fervent Jacobin advocate. He ended up being the man who saved France from total annihilation at the hands of the extremists and turned his back on the *Ancien Régime* of the Royalists.

The events leading up to his seizure of power can be understood by examining the chain of events set in motion by the Terror and the corruption within the Directory. His declaration as emperor can also be seen as a response to the circumstances at the time— a means to stabilize the government, deter conspiracies, and reinstate order. However, his ambitions went beyond this.

Shortly after becoming consul, Napoleon concentrated all the power in his hands and established an autocratic regime similar to the absolute monarchy that the revolution had overthrown. Did the French people pay an excessively high price for internal peace? Furthermore, Napoleon spread the effects of the French Revolution across all of Europe, and later the whole world. Were the Napoleonic Wars too costly for humankind to ensure the principles of liberty, equality, and fraternity?

On the other hand, Napoleon introduced a series of positive reforms to modernize the feudal system in France. If France wanted to remain a power in Europe, it had to keep pace with the countries that had entered the Industrial Revolution. The abolition of the Estate System was just the beginning. A modern country needs new infrastructure, a suitable legal frame, and an updated state administration system. Napoleon must be credited for doing all of that. Without the French Revolution, medieval France would have probably endured for many years, and it is hard to imagine what would have happened if Napoleon hadn't supported the revolution.

Napoleon provided the legal structures and invested to modernize the state. He introduced the Napoleonic Code, one of the first comprehensive legal systems that established equality before the law and civil liberties. It served as the basis for many European countries' legal systems, and then, European influence spread it across the globe.

He concentrated his power as an emperor and ensured nothing could challenge it, but he also empowered citizens by turning ideals into laws. These laws became the foundation of a global legal system: "The Napoleonic Code has been adopted by dozens of nations around the world. The Code forbade birthright privilege, granted freedom of religion, and specified that government jobs should be awarded on merit alone" (James, 2018, para. 12).

Besides the implementation of the Code, Napoleon was a statesman. Despite being an emperor, he showed people he cared for them. Public opinion mattered. It might have been to build popular support for his own figure, but the quality of life of the common citizen improved. It was a characteristic that distinguished his regime from other autocratic regimes.

Napoleon also established a new public education system and a tax code. Furthermore, he made public investments in roads and sewer systems. He also defined a new role for the state in the economy by creating the first central bank in French history.

On the other hand, it must be pointed out that Napoleon ruled with an iron fist. He knew the power of ideas and how quickly they spread through the press, so he used propaganda to his benefit while suppressing the freedom of speech of his opponents. He used censorship to control information about his government, and himself.

However, despite using all those instruments to consolidate his power, "he was also able to look beyond partisan and ideological divisions if he recognized exceptional skills and talents that could support his vision of France. The most illustrative example of this phenomenon is his collaboration with Charles Maurice de Talleyrand" (*Napoleon's Government*, n.d., para. 5).

His personal ambitions were also an expression of his tyranny, and his success was enabled by that tyranny. He used military campaigns to expand his domains even though it meant mobilizing thousands of men on battlefields where they would die, suffer horrific wounds, and succumb to hunger and disease. Still, the French followed and supported him.

This was evidenced when he came back from Elba and quickly enlisted a massive number of volunteer soldiers. Napoleon had been cunning enough to equate his image with the national interest. These soldiers risked their lives for the glory of their nation, and perhaps for their leader.

However, thousands of men from the occupied or subjugated nations were also dragged to battle during the Napoleonic Wars. They had to fight for the empire that subjugated them, and they didn't have a choice. Besides, the people of France were compelled to allocate resources that should have been used to improve their quality of life to military campaigns that pursued Napoleon's personal goals. Moreover, the empire imposed heavy taxation to increase public incomes destined to finance Napoleon's ambitions.

Bonaparte and Other Historical Figures

It is inevitable to compare Napoleon with other prominent figures who left a mark in history. It is difficult to set the parameters to address such a comparison since each historical figure developed in a unique context. It would be impossible to predict how they would perform if they were placed in other scenarios.

For instance, Napoleon is usually compared to Julius Caesar and Alexander the Great. However, it is hard to guess how Napoleon would have dealt with the Roman Senate in a well-established (if corrupt) republic. Or, how he would have prevented the disintegration of his empire as it happened with the Macedonian Empire of Alexander.

However, there are several aspects that can be compared between them. They were all leaders with great visions for their empires, and all faced significant opposition from rival factions. They are also remembered for their military strategy, governance, and political leadership, and the enduring influence they left on their nations and humankind's history.

Julius Caesar's military career bloomed late, but burned bright. And he had better personal political skills than Napoleon; he was, after all, a Roman to the core, not an outsider. He led the expansion of Rome even in times of the Republic. It was triggered by social unrest, but not at the levels of the French crisis before the revolution. His military and political genius allowed him to take Rome outside the limits of the Republic. He would have ruled the Roman Empire if he hadn't been assassinated (Duch, 2020). Napoleon was in a different situation. Nonetheless, he had the ability to anticipate events. There were many conspiracies to kill him, and still he managed to settle alliances and deploy strategies to prevail.

On the other hand, Napoleon's empire wasn't as extensive as Alexander's. The Macedonian captain-general-turned-king had a unique talent to lead his army on the battlefield and to administer the conquered territories. However, he failed to provide his kingdom with a solid basis that could endure beyond his premature death. He was strong, but his empire was weak. After his death, the empire was torn down to ruins. Instead, Napoleon left an enduring legacy in all of Europe.

Napoleon's Code provided a political and legal frame to an empire that hosted people of different roots and could all benefit from it. "Without his failure in the campaign against the Russian Empire, the European continent today could have been the 'European Empire' with a monarchical system or the 'United States of Europe' with democracy" (Duch, 2020, para. 14). In a sense, the ideal of a unified Europe under a unified legal system and a central power to ensure peace remains culturally and politically relevant.

Chapter Overview

Autocratic regimes and popular interests are two opposing concepts, and it is fair to wonder if they can coexist. Many political changes can only be achieved through violent and costly processes. The Napoleonic Wars were perhaps a high price to pay for the consolidation of liberal ideas. Napoleon's despotism can be considered an inevitable moment of struggle in humankind's path to progress. However, the abuse of power and the hundreds of thousands of casualties in Europe were the costly outcomes of his ambition.

How many ordinary people's lives can be sacrificed in the name of progress? Can one great man lead and decide that? Should history exalt his name or condemn him? Those questions remain open whenever we look at Napoleon's era. However, he did enough to invite us to revisit his life and work.

As we've explored Napoleon's personal life and the many facets of his rule, we are left with a lingering question: Was Napoleon's success the product of exceptional genius, or was it more the result of fortunate circumstances? In the next chapter, we will dive deeper into Napoleon's leadership style, examining his military strategies, governance, and reforms.

Chapter 11: Napoleon's Leadership: Genius or Luck?

I would rather have a general who was lucky than one who was good. –Napoleon Bonaparte

Napoleon Bonaparte is known for his audacious strategies and lightning-fast campaigns. Yet, some argue that luck played a significant role in his conquests. Was he truly a military genius, or just a fortunate gambler?

A thorough analysis of the most important battles fought by Napoleon allows us to see that luck is only fruitful when there is a leader who can read the circumstances properly and make the right decisions. Therefore, luck is a skill if it is used properly. There were several contextual features that enabled Napoleon to carry out his military campaigns and deploy innovative strategies. He seized power during the first decades of the Industrial Revolution and took advantage of an increased production capacity. Meanwhile, the internal crisis and the continuous changes in the government of France enabled him to manipulate financial resources and industrial production, directing them to his military affairs. This allowed Napoleon to count on a better-equipped army.

On the other hand, one of the most important changes introduced by Napoleon to modern warfare was the increase of the size of the army by conscription: "From 1800-1811, Napoleon raised 1.3 million conscripts and 1 million more from 1812-1813" (Chavous, n.d., para. 12). The historical context favored him, as Napoleon used the French Revolution and the threat of a foreign invasion to fuel nationalist sentiment.

Also, he reinforced the role the army played in enabling social promotion, much as Napoleon had benefitted himself. For instance, he implemented a system of promotion based on the soldiers' performance on the battlefield. It allowed more men to improve their lives significantly, increased the level of professionalization of the army, and grew Napoleon's popularity.

Nonetheless, having such a large army made it difficult to supply them. It also made it hard to lead them properly on the battlefield. He had to make them move quickly and use them judiciously on the battlefield to administer the resources sparingly.

Then, he introduced innovative formations of the infantry, such as column and line formations and infantry squares. He made clever use of cavalry and artillery like cannons, howitzers, and guns. He also introduced the tactic of separating his forces and then attacking by the flanks.

However, he had the ability to control the flow of communication among the divisions and present a coordinated attack. The success at the Battle of Austerlitz was achieved thanks to the excellent timing and communication to make all the divisions take their assigned places and roles in the battle. This wouldn't have worked if the groups didn't have efficient generals, and if there had not been a clear and strong command led by Bonaparte himself.

The divisions could perform perfectly as individual units or as instruments of the same orchestra. The key to Napoleon's success in leading a massive army was having decisions and orders concentrated in his own power; but at the same time, he effectively transmitted them through the different levels of military hierarchy until they reached every rank of the soldiery. On the battlefield, everybody knew what to do.

In addition to this, Napoleon had a perfect understanding of the role played by natural features such as the terrain and weather conditions. It was proven, again at Austerlitz, and during his first triumph against Prussia. Yet, his frustrated campaign against Russia and his defeat at Leipzig was a result of these factors, but mainly due to an unexpected shift during the battle. Napoleon's influence also motivated innovations in the enemy's army. He reshaped warfare, but eventually, the changes he introduced turned against him.

One of the most challenging obstacles he had to deal with was the logistic support for such a large army. He couldn't depend on supplies that could be taken by the army to the battlefront. Therefore, he paid special attention to the available resources in the country he invaded. This determined the path his army followed towards Russia.

To obtain enough food for his troops, he trained his men to forage during campaigns. By the beginning of the 19th century, Europe was going through a new stage of agricultural revolution. Therefore, there were crops everywhere, and French soldiers took what they found on their path.

The Delicate Balance Between Genius and Luck

Napoleon's military genius can't be judged by the number of victories or defeats on the battlefield. It also can't be ignored that he faced only a few categorical defeats which marked a turning point in his empire. While he collected many triumphs, the defeats in Leipzig and Waterloo were enough to end the Empire. However, this doesn't overshadow his superb talent on the battlefield, especially considering the great risks he dared to take to achieve his goals:

> His military and diplomatic strategy was offensive, quick, and decisive. Numerous times he successfully maneuvered to divide a unified enemy and then picked each off individually. He used fear to impose peace, concluded treaties with countries who had seen his power, used the media to spread his message, and worked to prevent or split coalitions (The Raab Collection, 1969, para. 1).

The difference between being a genius or not isn't necessarily defined by success. Napoleon could control internal commotion in France, restoring order, and building an empire against which a whole continent would rise up in opposition. In those terms, his genius is unquestionable. Luck can allow triumph, but Napoleon was able to manage and lead conflicts and processes without it.

Moreover, Napoleon's lessons about strategy transcended time. Even today, his strategies are studied in military colleges all over the world, and his lessons about strategy are implemented in every field. Some of the most remarkable are:

- The use of deception to create favorable advantages
- Speed and mobility
- Ability to organize logistics and supply
- Versatility and adaptability
- A decisive attitude
- Knowing the rival and anticipating their moves
- The effective use of the available resources
- Planning
- Leadership on the front
- The value of morale and motivation

Napoleon's leadership was characterized by his decisive attitude and rational, accurate readings of the circumstances. That shouldn't be considered a stroke of luck; Napoleon's enemies were in the same circumstances, and (generally speaking) they could not use them to a similar advantage. His greatest virtue as a genius, however, was his distinctive adaptability and ability to learn from his mistakes. He was bold and determined, but never hesitated to adjust his strategies whenever it was needed.

Chapter Overview

Napoleon once famously said: "Never interrupt your enemy when he is making a mistake." Despite his genius, the other players on the European board also played, and they had learned from Napoleon. Like him, other European armies also resorted to conscription to enlarge their numbers and used public taxation and funds to increase expenditures on military supplies. Every time Napoleon let the world know about his power, he elicited a new approach among his enemies. Every time he deployed a new strategy, he exposed his virtues, but also his weaknesses, and his opponents finally capitalized.

He attempted to build a unified Europe under one power. It might have brought enduring peace; it certainly boosted a new balance of power. But instead of unity, it enhanced fragmentation. Peace became a primary goal for all the powers; but still, nations searched to ensure their own positions.

Napoleon's leadership was undeniably transformative; it was also highly controversial. His rule left a lasting impact on Europe and the world; an impact that still resonates today. In the last chapter, we will explore the enduring legacy of Napoleon and the shadow he casts over modern history. We will assess how his influence shaped the political, military, and cultural landscape of Europe, and how his memory is still invoked in contemporary debates and discussions.

Chapter 12: The Legacy and Shadow of Napoleon

The Napoleonic Code, which Napoleon introduced in 1804, forms the basis of modern civil law in many countries around the world.

Napoleon was moved by personal ambitions and a nationalist interest. However, his legacy reached much further than the borders of his empire. As explained in the previous chapter, his innovative strategies in the military field had extensive consequences in warfare. The European states changed their view of their armies and the way to fight wars also evolved. On the other hand, diplomatic relationships and the balance of power changed as another direct consequence of Napoleon's empire and political leadership.

The Congress of Vienna was designed by Prince Metternich for the purpose of preventing any future possibility of a new Napoleonic empire. Napoleon was defeated after 15 years of attempts by the greatest powers of Europe to destabilize France.

Leipzig was perceived as a triumph by the allies, but Napoleon had forced them to introduce a new way of perceiving the balance of power on the continent. It was the first time in history that the key players of the international board were summoned to decide how they would ensure peace. It is one of the most important precedents of international diplomatic relationships.

It was challenging to create an institution that would regulate the relationship among states. There weren't similar experiences in the past to follow, and there was no way to predict the outcomes. One of the hot questions was who should participate in such an institution. Should France and its traditional monarchy be included in the negotiations? France was the reason why Europe was dragged into wars for over 15 years—should the nation be invited to arrange peace? Was it enough that Napoleon was removed from the political scenario, or did the French nation as a whole have the same objectives as the deposed emperor?

In the end, it was decided that the four winners would decide the future: Prussia, Austria, Great Britain, and Russia. There were historical rivalries among them, and they especially distrusted the Russian tsar. Nevertheless, if they wanted to prevent a new leader from starting more expansionist wars, it was best to include him at the small table of negotiators.

The summit was arranged to take place in Vienna (after all, it had been Metternich's idea) on September 22, 1814. The decisions would later be announced to France and Spain, the latter of which was dealing with its own war in America. However, the representatives of the countries arrived in Vienna at the end of September: Prince von Metternich represented Emperor Francis II; Prince von Hardenberg represented King Frederick William III of Prussia, and Viscount

Castlereagh from Great Britain. Tsar Alexander I of Russia directed his own diplomacy (Encyclopaedia Britannica, 2023).

The fundamentals of the Congress of Vienna were to forbid any European nation from becoming so strong as to threaten the peace in the continent. In the preceding period, national interest had been valued over any other diplomatic principle. After Napoleon, such a policy was perceived as dangerous; nations would hurry to ally, and national security would be seriously threatened. The focus couldn't only be put on what a state could do, but also on what it would lead the other powers to do.

The other key purpose of the Congress of Vienna was to strengthen Central Europe. In ancient times, when Central Europe was unified, Charlemagne (and later the Holy Roman Empire) addressed the desire to unify Europe under one single empire, subverting nationalist tendencies. On the other hand, when Central Europe was fragmented, it offered a tempting target for the expansionist pretensions of other great powers such as France, or Russia. No nation should be so weak as to become an easy target for any other power.

Great Britain had preserved its policy of non-interventionism in continental affairs for centuries. After Napoleon, Great Britain understood that the continental union had put the country's supremacy at risk.

Once France was forced to retreat to its limits before Napoleon's expansionist campaigns, the Congress of Vienna decided on new limits for the European territories. Russia claimed the possession of Poland. In return, it gave back Galicia to Austria, which obtained Venice and Lombardy and further territories in present-day Germany. The rest of Italy remained separated in minor principalities.

Prussia obtained Saxony, Westphalia, and the west side on the bank of the Rhine River. The Kingdom of the Netherlands was created at the behest of Great Britain, and it gathered the provinces of Belgium and Holland as a preventive frontier between Prussia and France. Denmark lost its power over Norway which was annexed by Sweden, and Hannover was enlarged.

On June 9, 1815, the final act was signed by the four major powers and four other nations were added later (France, Spain, Sweden, and Portugal): "The statesmen had successfully worked out the principle of a balance of power. However, the idea of nationality had been almost entirely ignored—necessarily so because it was not yet ready for expression" (Encyclopaedia Britannica, 2023, para. 12). It was an effective measure at the time, but it triggered nationalist conflicts that eventually challenged the central empires: World War I.

The Moral Ambivalence of Genius

Napoleon Bonaparte was an emperor who pursued the ancient idea of putting all the power under one single crown. The ideal of the universal empire motivated the Roman Caesars and Alexander the Great in Ancient times, but also Charlemagne and the Holy Roman Empire in the Medieval period. It was an ideal that was supposed to ensure peace and progress. It resulted in war, death, and conflict.

Napoleon's ideals and personal ambitions took France into an era of military supremacy. However, the devastating defeats at the end nearly destroyed the nation's army and left it in a weak position. That said, Napoleon left enduring institutions within France, such as the judicial system, the central bank, a new and modern educational system, centralized universities, and the Napoleonic Code. He changed the history of his country and the whole world (Encyclopaedia Britannica, 2020).

Historians and scholars have painted Napoleon from diametrically opposed perspectives. For some, he was a hero. For others, he was a tyrant. The treatment history gives different figures and periods is strongly influenced by current circumstances. It is not the same to think about the French Revolution in times of social upheaval or the risk of social disintegration in moments of prosperity and stability. The perspectives on Napoleon also fluctuate, even in France:

> Nobody talks about him in schools anymore. It's worse than being detested, he is ignored, and yet Bonaparte had a stunning history [...]. Many French see him as representing a war-mongering, authoritarian regime and forget the many things we inherited from him, including his great administrative reorganization (Willsher, 2017, para. 7).

The question of how history should judge Napoleon has divided scholars and the French community for over 200 years. The positive or negative evaluations of his leadership and military campaigns are also used for political purposes. Some scholars claim that in the present, there is a politically correct way to judge him.

Autocratic traits from his government are highlighted in his achievements and reforms. For instance, he is strongly condemned for introducing slavery to the Caribbean and the islands in the Indian Ocean, his dictatorship, and his aggressive foreign policy. However, scholars also claim that none of these were completely out of line with the policies of neighboring countries (Williamson, 2021).

Therefore, many modern historians attempt to strike a balance by considering both the positive and negative aspects of Napoleon's rule. He is depicted as an emperor, a military leader, and a politician, but also as a man. At the present, history attempts to study the past by observing, and accepting, the light and dark sides of every great figure.

Chapter Overview

The Congress of Vienna was the direct aftermath of the Napoleonic Wars and the ultimate defeat of Napoleon at Waterloo. It meant the restoration of the monarchy and the stabilization of the traditional system in Europe. However, nothing was the same on the continent, and in the long term, the consequences of the Napoleonic legacy would reach the 21st century. The impact of the reshaping of Europe and the shift in the logic of international relationships endure to the present.

As we've explored Napoleon's life, military conquests, political leadership, and lasting legacy, it's become evident that he was a man of both genius and ambition. As we conclude this book, let's reflect on the lessons we can learn from his rise and fall, and how his influence continues to shape the world.

Conclusion

There are only two forces in the world: the sword and the spirit. In the long run, the sword will always be conquered by the spirit. –Napoleon Bonaparte

Two centuries after his death, Napoleon continues to be a subject of interest. His work left a significant impact on history regarding military conquest, the development of modern warfare, and political reforms, including international diplomacy. His life was framed by the French Revolution, one of the processes that set the stage for the beginning of a new era, and he was one of the men who helped to build it.

His personal life is as interesting as his public career. A young boy from a small nation became the most respected and feared leader in the world; a ruler of one of the most powerful empires in history. He represents the triumph of will over circumstance and is also an example of how genius can coexist with unlimited ambition. His superb leadership was poisoned with his irrepressible ambition and thirst for glory.

Even though the purpose of this book is to address Napoleon's image from different perspectives, without any bias, it is inevitable to emphasize either the positive or the negative aspects of his leadership, his goals, and the means he used to achieve them. Historians and scholars face the challenge of bringing Napoleon's legacy into the 21st century to learn from him, revisit his ideals and methods, and reflect upon the consequences for which he was responsible. Indeed, it is an interesting exercise to ponder whether you consider him a hero or a tyrant; a product or the architect of the circumstances that framed his life.

As we conclude our exploration of Napoleon's life, it is essential to reflect on the lessons it offers. After reading these pages, you have enough resources to think about your initial perception of Napoleon and how it may have changed after delving into his story.

The strategies and leadership traits exhibited by Napoleon can serve as a source of inspiration in our professional lives. He proved it is possible to dream big and use circumstances in your favor. His life is an example of what sheer strength of will can accomplish.

This book is also an invitation to take those lessons from this remarkable character. Think about the ways you adapt to changing circumstances, and how you might use lessons from his life to enhance your adaptability. By doing so, we can glean valuable insights from history to shape our own experiences.

We must all reflect on the past to learn from history. A deeper understanding of how and why the world we live in developed the way it did will help prevent us from repeating the mistakes of the past and empower us to keep improving our lives. Napoleon was a great man who left an enduring mark on humankind's history, but every one of us is making our own contribution.

Note to the Reader

Providing sincere feedback is the best way to support (and improve) the work of independent publishers. If you enjoyed and found value in this book, please leave a review and invite others to learn about and reflect upon our common past to build a promising future.

Scan the code to leave a review!

Glossary

abdication. The act of resigning from a monarchic or similar position, something Napoleon did twice in his life.

artillery. Large-caliber guns used in warfare on land.

battle formations. Strategic placements of troops in battle, such as squares, lines, or columns.

cavalry. Soldiers or warriors who fight mounted on horseback.

Coalition Wars. A series of wars where different European states teamed up against France during Napoleon's rule.

consulship. The highest elected political office during the Roman Republic, which Napoleon adopted as a title during his rule.

Continental System. An economic strategy employed by Napoleon to paralyze Great Britain through the control of European ports.

Corsican Republic. The nation on the island of Corsica, where Napoleon was born.

coup d'état. A sudden and decisive action in politics, usually resulting in a change of government by illegal or forceful means.

Elba and Saint Helena. Islands where Napoleon was exiled.

Grande Armée. Napoleon's main military force, which he led in numerous campaigns throughout Europe.

guerrilla warfare. A form of irregular warfare where small groups use military tactics like ambushes to combat larger and less mobile armies.

infantry. Soldiers who march and fight on foot.

Napoleonic Code. A legal code established by Napoleon that served as a model for many countries' civil law systems.

siege. A military blockade and assault of a city or fortress with the intent of capturing it.

References

A-Z Quotes. (n.d.). *"I would rather have a general who was lucky than one who was good."* https://www.azquotes.com/quote/1339632

Abate, J.S. (1995). *Napoleonic Propaganda: Rationalization for War and Control of an Empire.* Utah State University. https://digital-commons.usu.edu/cgi/viewcontent.cgi?article=1394&context=honors

Abel, G.M. (2021, April 7). *Austerlitz, the battle of the three emperors.* National Geographic. https://historia.nationalgeo-graphic.com.es/a/austerlitz-batalla-tres-emperadores_16596

Altenhof, A. (n.d.). *The Napoleonic Wars: cause, effects and battles.* StudySmarter. https://www.studysmarter.co.uk/explana-tions/history/the-french-revolution/napoleonic-wars/

Andrews, E. (1896). *Napoleon's alleged epilepsy.* JAMA Network. https://jamanetwork.com/journals/jama/arti-cle-abstract/459819

Baron François Gérard (1770-1837) - Jérôme Bonaparte, King of Westphalia (1784-1860). (n.d.). Royal Collection Trust. https://www.rct.uk/col-lection/406371/jerome-bonaparte-king-of-westphalia-1784-1860#:~:text=Description

Battle of Aboukir Bay. (2006, June 12). HistoryNet. https://www.historynet.com/battle-of-aboukir-bay/

Bonaparte saves the day. (n.d.). Liberty, Equality, Fraternity: Exploring the French Revolution. https://revolution.chnm.org/d/451

Boudon, J.O. (n.d.). *Why St. Helena?* Napoleon.org. https://www.napoleon.org/en/history-of-the-two-empires/articles/why-st-helena/

BrainyQuotes. (n.d.). *Napoleon Bonaparte - I love power. But it is as an artist...* https://www.brainyquote.com/quotes/napoleon_bonaparte_150182

BrainyQuotes. (n.d.). *Napoleon Bonaparte - The strong man is the one who is able...* https://www.brainyquote.com/quotes/napoleon_bonaparte_150174#google_vignette

BrainyQuotes. (n.d.). *Napoleon Bonaparte - There are only two forces in the...* https://www.brainyquote.com/quotes/napoleon_bonaparte_118625

Brooks, I., Fox-Martin, A. & Van der Colff, S. (2020, May 26). *History grade 10 - Topic 3 essay Questions.* South African History Online. https://www.sahistory.org.za/article/history-grade-10-topic-3-essay-questions#:~:text=%5B1%5D%20The%20French%20revolution%20occurred

Chavous, J. (n.d.). Saddles and sabers: Napoleon Bonaparte's contributions to modern warfare.

eArmor. https://www.moore.army.mil/ar-
mor/earmor/content/issues/2014/MAR_JUN/
Chavous.html

Chevalier, B. (2009). *Napoleon Bonaparte, student
of the Royal Military School in Brienne, aged 15
years old*. Napoleon.org. https://www.napo-
leon.org/en/history-of-the-two-
empires/objects/napoleon-bonaparte-student-
of-the-royal-military-school-in-brienne-aged-
15-years-old/

Clark, M., Knights, M.F., Wickham, C.J., Marino,
J.A., Foot, J., Larner, J., Lovett, C.M., Palma,
G.D., Signoretta, P.E., Berengo, M., Palma, G.D.,
King, R.L., Nangeroni, G. & Powell, J.M. (2023,
October 2). *Italy*. Encyclopedia Britannica.
https://www.britannica.com/place/Italy

Clendenin, C. (2022, April 11). *The rise of Napoleon
Bonaparte: Overview and reforms*. Study.com.
https://study.com/learn/lesson/napoleon-bo-
naparte-empire-early-reforms.html

Cuccia, P.R. (n.d.). *Napoleon in Italy: The Siege of
Mantua, 1796-1799*. Napoleon.org.
https://www.napoleon.org/en/magazine/publi-
cations/napoleon-in-italy-the-sieges-of-
mantua-1796-1799/

De Cleen, M. (2022, December 20). *A French king
in Holland*. Mfor Amsterdam Tours.
https://mforamsterdam.com/a-french-king-in-
holland/

Duch, L. (2020, January 9). Alexander Vs. Julius Caesar Vs. Napoléon: Julius Augustus as the greatest military commander — EVER. Search Medium. https://medium.com/@lalin.matt/alexander-caesar-napol%C3%A9on-julius-augustus-as-the-greatest-military-commander-ever-407a911255db

1804 - Napoleon proclaimed Emperor in France. (n.d.). Keats-Shelley House. https://ksh.roma.it/romanticism/1804

1813 and the lead up to the Battle of Leipzig. (2013). Napoleon.org. https://www.napoleon.org/en/history-of-the-two-empires/timelines/1813-and-the-lead-up-to-the-battle-of-leipzig/

Encyclopaedia Britannica. (2011, November 24). *Consulate.* https://www.britannica.com/topic/Consulate-French-history

Encyclopaedia Britannica. (2020, October 16). *Napoleon I's Achievements.* https://www.britannica.com/summary/Napoleon-Is-Achievements

Encyclopaedia Britannica. (2020, January 19). *Continental System.* https://www.britannica.com/event/Continental-System

Encyclopaedia Britannica. (2022, October 21). *Estates-General.* https://www.britannica.com/topic/Estates-General

Encyclopaedia Britannica. (2022, December 19). *Treaty of Pressburg*. https://www.britannica.com/event/Treaty-of-Pressburg-1805

Encyclopaedia Britannica. (2023, October 17). *Reign of Terror*. https://www.britannica.com/event/Reign-of-Terror

Encyclopaedia Britannica. (2023, June 9). *Battle of Leipzig*. https://www.britannica.com/event/Battle-of-Leipzig

Encyclopaedia Britannica. (2023, July 8). *Treaties of Tilsit*. https://www.britannica.com/topic/Treaties-of-Tilsit

Encyclopaedia Britannica. (2023, July 21). *Battle of the Pyramids*. https://www.britannica.com/event/Battle-of-the-Pyramids-Egyptian-history

Encyclopaedia Britannica. (2023, August 13). *Prussia*. https://www.britannica.com/place/Prussia

Encyclopaedia Britannica. (2023, August 19). *Louis Bonaparte*. https://www.britannica.com/biography/Loui)s-Bonaparte-king-of-Holland

Encyclopaedia Britannica. (2023, August 22). *Congress of Vienna*. https://www.britannica.com/event/Congress-of-Vienna

Encyclopaedia Britannica. (2023, August 31). *Peninsular War*. https://www.britannica.com/event/Peninsular-War

Encyclopaedia Britannica. (2023, September 8). *Battle of Austerlitz.* https://www.britannica.com/event/Battle-of-Austerlitz

Encyclopaedia Britannica. (2023, September 19). *French Revolution.* https://www.britannica.com/event/French-Revolution

Encyclopaedia Britannica. (2023, September 20). *Napoleonic Wars.* https://www.britannica.com/event/Napoleonic-Wars

Encyclopaedia Britannica. (2023, September 27). *Battle of Waterloo.* https://www.britannica.com/event/Battle-of-Waterloo

Feloni, R. (2014, August 4). 7 Management strategies from some of history's greatest generals. Insider. https://www.businessinsider.com/war-strategies-for-management-2014-8#:~:text=%22The%20moral%20is%20to%20the

Fid Backhouse & others. (2023, September 23). French invasion of Russia. Encyclopaedia Britannica. https://www.britannica.com/event/French-invasion-of-Russia

Gifford, J. (2012, April 1). *Napoleon's whiff of grapeshot.* Jonathangifford.com. https://jonathangifford.com/napoleons-whiff-of-grapeshot/

Glossary of war of 1812 terms. (n.d.). American Battlefield Trust. https://www.battlefields.org/glossary-war-1812-terms

Godechot, J. (2023, September 27). *Napoleon I.* Encyclopaedia Britannica.

https://www.britannica.com/biography/Napoleon-I

Goodreads. (n.d.). Quote by Napoleon Bonaparte: "Impossible is the word found only in a fool's d…" https://www.goodreads.com/quotes/714108-impossible-is-the-word-found-only-in-a-fool-s-dictionary

Graves, D. (2006). *French military terminology 1670 - 1815: a Technical glossary.* French Military Terminology 1670 - 1815: a Technical Glossary

Greenspan, J. (2023, August 11). TITLE. History Channel. www.history.com/news/napoleons-disastrous-invasion-of-russia -MM

Harrison, R.J., O'Callaghan, J.F., Smith, C.D., Viguera, M.J., Richardson, J.S., Ginés, J.V., Koenigsberger, H.G., Carr, R., Rodriguez, V. & Shubert, A. (2023, September 24). *Spain.* Encyclopaedia Britannica. https://www.britannica.com/place/Spain.

Hicks, P. (n.d.). Russia and France The messy break-up… Napoleon.org. https://www.napoleon.org/en/history-of-the-two-empires/articles/russia-and-france-the-messy-break-up/

Hughes, J.R. (2003, December 4). Emperor Napoleon Bonaparte: did he have seizures?

Psychogenic or epileptic or both? *Epilepsy Behav,* 4(6):793-6. doi: 10.1016/j.yebeh.2003.09.005

Invasion of Russia. (n.d.). Lumen Learning. https://courses.lumenlearning.com/suny-hccc-worldhistory2/chapter/invasion-of-russia/

Italy under Napoleon | History of Western Civilization II. (n.d.). Lumen Learning. https://courses.lumenlearning.com/suny-hccc-worldhistory2/chapter/italy-under-napoleon/

James, D. (2018, May 1). *Napoleon: Hero or Tyrant?* 5-Minute History. https://fiveminutehistory.com/napoleon-hero-or-tyrant/

Knight, J. (2012, December 11). Napoleon wasn't defeated by the Russians. Slate. https://slate.com/technology/2012/12/napoleon-march-to-russia-in-1812-typhus-spread-by-lice-was-more-powerful-than-tchaikovskys-cannonfire.html

Knighton, A. (2017, December 24). *The meat grinder of war – Why the Napoleonic Wars cost so many lives.* War History Online. https://www.warhistoryonline.com/napoleon/napoleonic-wars-cost.html

Lefevre, P. & Papot, E. (n.d.). *Napoleon in Egypt (2): The scientific expedition.* Napoleon.org. https://www.napoleon.org/en/young-historians/napodoc/bonaparte-in-egypt-2-the-scientific-expedition/

Lodi. (n.d.). Napoleon.org. https://www.napo-leon.org/en/magazine/places/lodi-2/

Lombardy, D. (2013). Napoleon's stunning debut: The Italian campaign. Warfare History Network. https://warfarehistorynetwork.com/article/na-poleons-stunning-debut-the-italian-campaign/

Louis, J. (n.d.). *Napoleon Forges an Empire*. CBSD. https://www.cbsd.org/cms/lib/PA01916442/Ce ntricity/Do-main/1907/ch%207%20sec%203%204%205.pd f

Lugli, A., Carneiro, F., Dawson, H., Fléjou, J.F., Kirsch, R., Van der Post, R.S., Vieth, M., Svrcek, M. (2021). The gastric disease of Napoleon Bonaparte: brief report for the bicentenary of Napoleon's death on St. Helena in 1821. *Virchows Arch.*, 479(5):1055-1060. doi: 10.1007/s00428-021-03061-1

Mark, H. (2022, July 14). *Napoleon Bonaparte during the early French Revolution (1789-1794)*. World History Encyclopedia. https://www.worldhistory.org/article/2036/na-poleon-bonaparte-during-the-early-french-revolut/

Mark, H. (2023, February 15). *Siege of Toulon*. World History Encyclopedia. https://www.worldhistory.org/arti-cle/2171/siege-of-toulon/

Mark, H. (2023, April 19). *Napoleon's Italian campaign*. World History Encyclopedia. https://www.worldhistory.org/Napoleon's_Italian_Campaign/

Mark, H. (2023, April 27). *Napoleon's campaign in Egypt and Syria. World History Encyclopedia.* https://www.worldhistory.org/Napoleon's_Campaign_in_Egypt_and_Syria/

Mark, H. (2023, May 18). *Coup of 18 Brumaire.* World History Encyclopedia. https://www.worldhistory.org/Coup_of_18_Brumaire/

Marlowe, L. (2020, January 20). *The mystery around Napoleon Bonaparte's father*. The Irish Times. https://www.irishtimes.com/news/world/europe/the-mystery-around-napoleon-bonapartes-father-1.4145818

Molinero, M.A. (2021, January 15). *Napoleon's military defeat in Egypt yielded a victory for history*. National Geographic. https://www.nationalgeographic.com/history/history-magazine/article/napoleon-military-defeat-egypt-yielded-victory-history#:~:text=Napoleon's%20military%20defeat%20in%20Egypt,became%20the%20foundation%20of%20Egyptology

Napoleon and Josephine - The Great Love Affair. (n.d.). French Cargo. https://frenchcargo.com.au/blogs/news/napoleon-and-josephine-the-great-love-

affair#:~:text=Jose-
phine%20was%20a%2032%2Dyear

Napoleon Bonaparte. (n.d.). Science, civilization, and society. http://www.phy-socean.icm.csic.es/science+society/lectures/illustrations/lecture21/napoleon.html

Napoleon Bonaparte. (2019, August 27). South African History Online. https://www.sahistory.org.za/article/napoleon-bonaparte

Napoleon's adieux to the Old Guard at Fontainebleau, 20 April, 1814. (n.d.). Napoleon.org. https://www.napoleon.org/en/history-of-the-two-empires/articles/napoleons-adieux-to-the-old-guard-at-fontainebleau-20-april-1814/

Napoleon: Napoleon at war. (n.d.). PBS. https://www.pbs.org/empires/napoleon/n_war/campaign/page_15.html

Napoleon's Government. (n.d.). Lumen Learning. https://courses.lumenlearning.com/suny-hccc-worldhistory2/chapter/napoleons-government/

Napoleon's Government: Further Centralization Of Power. (n.d.). Saylor Academy. https://learn.saylor.org/mod/book/view.php?id=54758&chapterid=40234

Napoleon's Rise to Power. (n.d.). Lumen Learning. https://courses.lumenlearning.com/suny-hccc-worldhistory2/chapter/napoleons-rise-to-power/#:~:text=Napoleon%20drew%20to-gether%20an%20alliance

The Napoleonic Code. (n.d.). Lumen Learning. https://courses.lumenlearning.com/suny-hccc-worldhistory2/chapter/the-napoleonic-code/

The Napoleonic Code: Legal System in France before the Code. (n.d.). Sailor Academy. https://learn.saylor.org/mod/book/view.php?id=54759&chapterid=40237#:~:text=Before%20the%20Napoleonic%20Code%2C%20France

The Napoleonic Invasion of Egypt. (n.d.). Napoleon and the Scientific Expedition to Egypt | Linda Hall Library. https://napoleon.linda-hall.org/learn.shtml#:~:text=Most%20famously%2C%20ancient%20Egypt%20was

Napoleonic Military Glossary. (n.d.). The Napoleonic Guide. https://www.napoleonguide.com/glossary.htm

National Army Museum. (n.d.). Peninsular War. https://www.nam.ac.uk/explore/peninsular-war#:~:text=Between%201808%20and%201814%2C%20the

National Gallery of Victoria (NGV). (n.d.). *Napoleon. Did you know?* https://www.ngv.vic.gov.au/napoleon/facts-and-figures/did-you-know.html

National Gallery of Victoria (NGV). (n.d.). Napoleon > Propaganda. https://www.ngv.vic.gov.au/napoleon/art-and-design/propaganda.html

National Gallery of Victoria (NGV). (n.d.). *Napoleon > The Italian Campaigns.* https://www.ngv.vic.gov.au/napoleon/facts-and-figures/the-italian-campaigns.html

National Gallery of Victoria (NGV). (n.d.). *Napoleon > Who was Josephine?* https://www.ngv.vic.gov.au/napoleon/napo-leon-and-josephine/who-was-josephine.html

National Gallery of Victoria (NGV). (n.d.). *Napoleon > Who's who?* https://www.ngv.vic.gov.au/na-poleon/facts-and-figures/whos-who.html

Niderost, E. (2022, February 28). Napoleon Bona-parte's failing health at Dresden. Warfare History Online. https://warfarehistorynet-work.com/napoleon-bonapartes-failing-health-at-dresden/#:~:text=Napo-leon%20won%20a%20great%20victory

Paris: Capital of the 19th Century. (n.d.). Brown University Library Center for Digital Scholar-ship. https://library.brown.edu/cds/paris/chronol-ogy2.html

Period glossary Archive. (n.d.). Napoleon.org. https://www.napoleon.org/en/magazine/pe-riod-glossary/

Peters, E. (2009). *The Napoleonic Egyptian scien-tific expedition and the ninetenth-century survey museum.* Seton Hall University.

https://scholarship.shu.edu/cgi/viewcon-
tent.cgi?article=1037&context=theses

Rijksmuseum. (n.d.). *Louis Napoleon Bonaparte.*
https://www.rijksmuseum.nl/en/rijksstu-
dio/historical-figures/louis-napoleon-bonaparte

Rouget, G. (n.d.). *Napoleon's Marriage to Marie-
Louise.* Lumen Learning. https://courses.lu-
menlearning.com/suny-hccc-
worldhistory2/chapter/napoleons-marriage-to-
marie-louise/

Rosetta Stone found | July 19, 1799. (2009). History
Channel. https://www.history.com/this-day-in-
history/rosetta-stone-found

Rothenberg, G. E. (1989). Soldiers and the Revolution: The French Army, Society, and the State,
1788-99 [Review of *The Army of the French
Revolution. From Citizen-Soldiers to Instrument of Power; Valmy ou la défense de la
nation pars les armes; The Bayonets of the Republic. Motivation and Tactics in the Army of
Revolutionary France, 1791-94; The Response
of the Royal Army to the French Revolution.
The Role and Development of the Line Army
1787-93*, by J.-P. Bertaud, R. R. Palmer, E. Hub-
lot, J. A. Lynn, & S. F. Scott]. *The Historical
Journal, 32*(4), 981–995.
http://www.jstor.org/stable/2639694

Scalf, F. (n.d.). *The Rosetta Stone: Unlocking the
ancient Egyptian language.* American Research
Center in Egypt. https://arce.org/resource/ro-
setta-stone-unlocking-ancient-egyptian-

language/#:~:text=The%20Ro-
setta%20Stone%2C%20a%20symbol

Schneid, F.C. (2011, January 27). *The French Revolutionary and Napoleonic Wars*. EGO.
http://ieg-ego.eu/en/threads/alliances-and-
wars/war-as-an-agent-of-transfer/frederick-c-
schneid-the-french-revolutionary-and-napole-
onic-wars

Sigler, J. (2011). *The Battle of Austerlitz and the
principles of war*. Napoleon.org.
https://www.napoleon.org/en/history-of-the-
two-empires/articles/the-battle-of-austerlitz-
and-the-principles-of-war/

SparkNotes. (n.d.). *Napoleon Bonaparte Study
Guide: Exile and Escape*.
https://www.sparknotes.com/biography/napo-
leon/section9/

SparkNotes. (n.d.). *Napoleon Bonaparte Study
Guide: Napoleon Becomes Emperor*.
https://www.sparknotes.com/biography/napo-
leon/section5/

Spary, S. (2021, January 7). *Rare doctor's note re-
veals Napoleon Bonaparte's poor health in
later years*. CNN. https://edi-
tion.cnn.com/2021/01/07/world/napoleon-
doctors-note-scli-intl/in-
dex.html#:~:text=The%20note%2C%20dated%
20June%204

Sun Tzu. (n.d.). *The Art of War.* https://web.stanford.edu/class/polisci211z/1.1/Sun%20Tzu.pdf

The Raab Collection. (1969, December 31). *Napoleon's grand military and diplomatic strategy: Divide the great powers; demonstrate strength; control negotiations.* https://www.raabcollection.com/napoleon-bonaparte-autograph/napoleon-bonaparte-signed-napoleons-grand-military-and-diplomatic

Timeline: Consulate/1st French Empire. (n.d.). Napoleon.org. https://www.napoleon.org/en/young-historians/napodoc/timeline-consulate1st-french-empire/

Wagnleitner, R.F., Holzner, L., Roider, K.A., Fellner, F., Leichter, O., Kirby, G.H., Stadler, Karl, R. and Zöllner, E. (2023, October 2). *Austria.* Encyclopedia Britannica. https://www.britannica.com/place/Austria

What key events and factors led to the French defeat at the Battle of Waterloo in 1815? (n.d.). Kinnu. https://kinnu.xyz/kinnuverse/history/battles/the-battle-of-waterloo/

Wheeler, H.F.B. (n.d.). *The story of Napoleon.* Heritage History. https://www.heritage-history.com/index.php?c=read&author=wheeler&book=napoleon&story=officer

Why the Battle of Austerlitz was Napoleon's greatest triumph. (n.d.). History Skills. https://www.historyskills.com/classroom/modern-history/austerlitz/

Williamson, L. (2021, May 5). Napoleon's incendiary legacy divides France 200 years on. BBC News. https://www.bbc.com/news/world-europe-56977769

Willsher, K. (2017, September 7). Cruel despot or wise reformer? Napoleon's two faces go on view. The Guardian. https://www.theguardian.com/world/2017/sep/03/napoleon-exhibition-museum-france-modern-civilisation

Image References

Bastien Nvs. (2020, October 27). *Building under a white sky during the day.* Unsplash.com. https://unsplash.com/es/fotos/j_K-8dQMQzk

Bogitw. (2016, March 16). *Malmaison Castle Napoleon France.* Pixabay.com. https://pixabay.com/photos/malmaison-castle-napoleon-france-1262027/

British Library. (2019, December 16). *People fighting.* Unsplash.com. https://unsplash.com/es/fotos/4FVTUC95znE

British Library. (2019, December 30). *Soldiers fighting.* Unsplash.com. https://unsplash.com/es/fotos/wKxk6ODFIlU

Diana van Ormondt. (2021, May 25). *Three men in a black and white suit holding a red smoke hose.* Unsplash.com. https://unsplash.com/es/fotos/ImydssfRpSg

Europeana. (2020, January 6). *Battle.* Unsplash.com. https://unsplash.com/es/fotos/vq1QaWgQtz4

Nicolas HIPPERT. (2020, June 3). *Picture in greyscale of the face of a man.* Unsplash.com. https://unsplash.com/es/fotos/71wxZqCDcNU

user1469083764. (2017, January 3). *Napoleon oil painting the coronation.* Pixabay.com. https://pixabay.com/photos/napoleon-oil-painting-the-coronation-1948529/

Venus Major. (2020, May 4). *Tuileries.* Unsplash.com. https://unsplash.com/es/fotos/t_QC6uu3gJM

WikiImages. (2012, December 4). *Napoleon Bonaparte emperor.* Pixabay.com. https://pixabay.com/illustrations/napoleon-bonaparte-emperor-62860/

WikiImages. (2012, December 19). France French Revolution. https://pixabay.com/es/fotos/francia-revoluci%C3%B3n-francesa-63022/

WikiImages. (2013, January 3). *Napoleon Bonaparte emperor France.* Pixabay.com. https://pixabay.com/photos/napoleon-bonaparte-emperor-france-67784/

WikiMediaImages. (2015, August 18). Napoleon Bonaparte portrait. Pixabay.com. https://pixabay.com/es/photos/napole%C3%B3n-bonaparte-retrato-884126/

www.ingramcontent.com/pod-product-compliance
Lightning Source LLC
Chambersburg PA
CBHW071354120626
46546CB00002B/691